Using Group-based Learning in Higher Education

EDITED BY

Lin Thorley and
Roy Gregory

**KOGAN
PAGE**

London • Philadelphia

Teaching and Learning in Higher Education Series
Series Editor: John Stephenson

First published in 1994

Kogan Page Limited
120 Pentonville Road
London N1 9JN

British Library Cataloguing in Publication Data

A CIP record for this book is available from the British Library.
ISBN 0 7494 1246 1

Typeset by Saxon Graphics Ltd, Derby.

Printed and bound in Great Britain by Biddles Ltd, Guildford and King's Lynn.

Contents

Acknowledgements

We would like to thank the following people and organizations for their part in producing this book:

Higher Education for Capability for running the 'Using Group-based Learning in Higher Education' conference from which most of the material has been drawn.

Enterprise in Higher Education at the University of Hertfordshire for their support for the conference.

Offley Place, Hitchin for hosting the conference.

Lynne Cunningham and Naomi Wilds for organizing the conference.

Cathy Crane, Lesley Bodman and Mary Corbett for help in preparing the manuscript.

The Contributors

Jon Baggott is a principal lecturer in personnel management at Thames Valley University. After training as a teacher, he moved into business studies teaching in further education and then into higher education. He is now responsible for several personnel management courses.

G S Bainbridge is presently divisional leader for chemical engineering at Teesside University. Responsible for the development of the MEng course in chemical engineering at Teesside, he has been an active participant in undergraduate teaching since 1968. He is also closely involved with the Institution of Chemical Engineers.

Michael Bramhall is a senior lecturer in materials engineering at Sheffield Hallam University. He is course leader for the integrated engineering degree. In addition to his research involvement in materials he has a strong interest in engineering and has numerous publications in this field.

Katherine Cuthbert lectures in psychology at the Crewe and Alsager Faculty of Manchester Metropolitan University. She teaches on a BA in applied social studies, an innovative degree scheme. She has a long–standing interest in student learning, particularly the promotion of students' intellectual and personal skills.

Peter Cuthbert is a senior lecturer in data processing at the Manchester Metropolitan University. He is course leader for the new BA business administration and is actively involved in the DMS and MSc management programmes. His research is mainly in teaching and learning in business and management studies.

Chris Dawson of Thames Valley University has been a lecturer in higher education for 15 years. Prior to that he had a successful career as a person-nel manager in the engineering industry. His current research interests include the effects of group composition on student learning, the basis for valuation of higher education by its main stakeholders and human resource accounting techniques.

Diane Garland is senior lecturer in human resource studies at Plymouth Business School, University of Plymouth. The UPshot programme has been featured by the author in a live satellite transmission to the Ukraine. Diane is currently researching into the issues involved in assessing group-work, acting as programme leader of a faculty-wide working party.

Annie Grant has been director of the Enterprise Learning Initiative at Leicester University since June 1991. Her previous career was in environmental archaeology. In the summer of 1993, she was appointed director of the careers and welfare service at Leicester, including overall responsibility for Enterprise.

Roy Gregory is a principal lecturer at the University of Hertfordshire. He is currently also learning development tutor for the school of engineering, where he has responsibility for developments in teaching and learning, group skills, and the teaching of personal transferable skills. He is also involved in staff development inside and outside the university, with a particular emphasis on learning and the effective use of groups.

Myszka Guzkowska is director of Enterprise in Higher Education at University College London. She has worked in a variety of organizations both as an academic and as a manager, and has an active interest in training, particularly in leadership, team-work, communication and project management skills.

Bob Harris has been teaching in further education and subsequently higher education for the past 13 years, and is now at Sheffield Hallam University. Previously, he worked in the steel industry as an engineer. He has particular interests in effective student group learning and the development of team skills.

Trevor Hassall and **Sarah Lewis** both lecture in accounting at Sheffield Hallam University. Their major research interest is the educational aspects of accounting and professional education. This currently focuses around the case study as a pedagogic device, group-based learning, and comparative studies of accounting education with other professional areas and in other countries.

Pamela Hunt is a senior lecturer in education at the University of Derby. She has taught in primary schools and worked as an advisory teacher. She was part of the development team for the Open University course 'Curriculum in action', an experience which led to her commitment to group learning based on observation.

Ivan Kent has been involved in training and development, primarily in the area of interpersonal and communication skills, for over 15 years. Since 1989 he has had a particular interest in student and staff development at UCL, where he is a member of the Enterprise in Higher Education team.

Patricia Lord is head of the school of management at Thames Valley University. Her teaching interests have focused on human resource management, while her research has been concerned with team building in the management context. She is joint author of textbooks in human resource management and of journal articles in the small and medium employer field.

Bob McGovern has taught in primary and secondary schools and has a particular interest in collaborative learning. He is currently a senior lecturer in education at the University of Derby.

Peter McHardy is an engineer and linguist with a background in international business development, in which he has held several directorships. He is currently a management consultant with Business Solutions of the De Montfort University, and a lecturer and author.

Jim McNally works in Enterprise in Higher Education at Glasgow University. Previous work includes freelance research, teaching in further and higher education, a secondment to the ILEA Curriculum Development Project – all following study as a mature student. Prior to entering higher education he worked in the engineering, building and haulage industries.

Brian Mathews is a senior lecturer in marketing at the University of Teesside Business School. For the past five years he has had responsibility for the development and operation of the Diploma in Management Studies group project. Over this time he has implemented a number of changes including the introduction of peer evaluation.

Geoff Nelder is manager of masters programmes at the CIM Institute, Cranfield University, where his duties include teaching and the supervision of industrial projects, with research interests in decision making in production planning and control. Prior to this he spent nine years in line management in the coal-mining industry.

Victor Newman teaches 'The learning organization' element of the masters degree at the CIM Institute, Cranfield University and has consultancy and research interests in problem solving, change management and team building, focused on the development and introduction of business improvement methodologies. He has experience of training and management development within MoD, Kodak and British Telecom.

David Nicholls is head of the school of history at the Manchester Metropolitan University. He has been responsible for a number of Enterprise projects, one of which, 'Independent study in history', was commended in the 1990 Partnership Awards. In addition to publishing accounts of these developments he also writes on 19th century history.

Martyn Pressnell is currently head of the aerospace engineering group at the University of Hertfordshire, where he teaches aircraft design and aerospace structures. He is also a consultant, being involved in Airship Industries product development, and has delivered several short lecture courses. He is a fellow of the Royal Aeronautical Society.

Graham Rawlinson is director of Enterprise in Higher Education at the University of Surrey and a chartered educational psychologist. He is an accredited trainer for the Synectics Education Initiative and author of the *Make it Count* basic numeracy workbook published by the National Extension College.

Ian Robinson followed a short career commission in the Navy by entering what is now Sheffield Hallam University where he has risen to become head of electrical and control engineering. His current interests are in the development of engineering education and the development of assessment by portfolio.

John Robson is a senior lecturer in the accounting and finance group at the University of Luton. He also has a long-term association as a part-time tutor with the Open University and is currently chair of the Open University Central Consultative Committee. His main interest is in the area of applications of soft systems methods.

Sneh Shah is currently scheme tutor at the University of Hertfordshire for a BEd degree designed for students with overseas qualifications. She is also manager of a project funded by the HEFCE to increase the number of minority ethnic teachers. She is active in learner-managed learning and is current editor of the journal of the World Education Fellowship.

Brian Stone is coordinator of management development in the department of business studies at the Manchester Metropolitan University. Previously in his career he has worked in advertising, then in business research at the

Manchester Business School, followed by a period as manager of management training courses at what is now the Royal Bank of Scotland.

Majorie Talbot was until recently senior lecturer in health studies at the University of East London. Her current interests are in health promotion development. She is now training the trainers in facilitation of group-management skills for the development of primary health care teams.

Lin Thorley is currently director of Enterprise in Higher Education at the University of Hertfordshire. She has been in education most of her working life, initially teaching biology then moving into the humanities. She now works as a practitioner in the development of personal skills and student-centred learning methods and is particularly active in group-based learning and in staff development.

Diana Tribe is professor of law at the University of Hertfordshire and associate research fellow at the Institute of Advanced Legal Studies, University of London. Her research and publications lie in the fields of legal education and medical law.

Judy Wilkinson is a lecturer in the department of electronics and electrical engineering at the University of Glasgow. She is currently involved in research into the teaching of mathematics to engineering students and with setting up a degree course in electronics for the environment.

Preface

The current interest in curriculum change sweeping through higher education – and further education – is a response to demands for the development of personal qualities and skills related to the world of work, ever-tightening resource constraints coupled with external assessments of the quality of provision, and the accumulation of awareness of good practice in teaching and learning. Indeed, much of our awareness of how further and higher education might be improved has been with us for some time. What is new is the commitment of institutions to introducing new practices across a wide range of their courses.

A major feature of these developments is an emphasis on the development of student autonomy in learning. Rapidly changing circumstances at work and in society are putting a premium on adaptability, working together and learning from experience. In the UK, national movements such as Higher Education for Capability (an initiative which originated in the Royal Society for the encouragement of Arts, Manufactures and Commerce (RSA) and is now based in Leeds Metropolitan University and the University of Leeds) and the Department of Employment's Enterprise in Higher Education initiative have stimulated much innovation. In Australasia, similar pressure for enhancing the quality and relevance of provision is provoking a similar response.

Interest in group-based learning is being driven by three major factors. First, there is a growing awareness, fuelled by criticisms from employers, that students need to be better equipped to work in teams and to be able to collaborate and communicate with people with specialisms other than their own. Second, pressures on staff resources are encouraging academics to explore ways in which students can work effectively in groups, perhaps without supervision. Third, academics and employers are becoming increasingly aware that collaborative learning can raise the quality of the learning experience by developing a range of personal skills and qualities, enhancing understanding of key concepts and giving exposure to a greater variety of perspectives and materials. It can also be fun.

The introduction of group-based learning has implications for students, academic staff, course design and assessment. For many teachers it implies the adoption of new roles and the use of techniques with which they may not be familiar. Making the case for group-based learning is one thing; giving people the confidence that they can do it is quite another.

Higher Education for Capability's 'Using...' series of publications is based on the proposition that there already exists a range of ways in which these new challenges are being met. The examples featured in this edition were presented at a national conference on using group-based learning organized by Higher Education for Capability, in association with the University of Hertfordshire and ICL Ltd. Some are well down the road, others are just starting out. We have included examples of both kinds since we anticipate readers will also be at different stages of development. We believe that others can learn from these experiences, particularly if new ideas and approaches are seen to be in operation and not just in somebody's imagination.

Part One of this book constitutes an overview of group-based learning. In Part Two, the largest section, we present a range of examples grouped under five themes: learning group skills, managing group learning, using group work to encourage student autonomy, case studies involving group work, and purpose-designed modules involving group work. Finally, in Part Three we present a review of this experience, including the issues raised, ways forward and the potential for further development.

This series will be of interest to all with responsibility for the design and delivery of the curriculum in higher and further education. We do not present blueprints or models of good practice but provide the reader with a glimpse of what others are doing and what they have learned from doing it, leaving readers to judge its relevance and adapt its implementation to their own circumstances. HEC would like to hear of other examples, particularly where they may better illustrate some of the issues raised by this book*. HEC publicizes examples in its National Capability and Enterprise Database which is available internationally via the Joint Academic Computer Network. The 'Using . . .' series is intended to be the start of an exchange of experience which might ultimately lead to greater understanding of the processes of teaching and learning in Higher and Further Education.

* Higher Education for Capability, 20 Queen Square, Leeds, LS2 8AF; telephone 0532 347725, facsimile 0532 442025.

Professor John Stephenson
Series Editor

Part One: The Context

Chapter One

Introduction

Roy Gregory and Lin Thorley

About this book

This is a book about group learning. It presents a snapshot of what is happening in higher education at the present time, produced by asking practitioners to write about their work.

Following a lengthy period of reluctance to exploit its possibilities, group-work is now firmly established in higher education. During the past few years group-based learning has not only become popular across a broad spectrum of disciplines but is also now used for increasingly varied and innovative learning purposes and situations.

This volume reflects this position. The contributors come from a wide variety of backgrounds and viewpoints. Part One: 'The Context' sets the scene in higher education. Part Two: 'The Experience' reports on activities some of which are still in pilot stage or under development, while others are relatively advanced. This is particularly helpful as it allows us as readers to benefit from colleagues' reflections and experiences at various stages of the learning and development cycle. This part of the book is in five sections. Sections One and Two deal with preparing students and identifying good tutor practice in running groups. Section Three covers the way groups can be used to encourage students as independent learners. Section Four presents a series of case studies of the way groups are being used within courses for project work, and Section Five reports on a number of purpose-designed modules using group-work. Finally, Part Three: 'Postscript' looks at some of the major issues that these contributions suggest we now face in group-based learning.

Using groups

We all use groups in higher education. There is a sense in which once we go beyond the individual tutorial we inevitably become involved in group-work. All gatherings for educational purposes, irrespective of size, have elements of group interaction which we may or may not use to advantage. Large lectures, small seminars and group-projects alike all provide us with the advantages and disadvantages inherent in social learning.

All too often, however, we as tutors do not think of the social learning aspects of methods such as lectures, or even seminars: we think of learning as group-based only when we intend consciously to exploit the social learning (as with group-projects) and when we as tutors will withdraw at least partially, leaving the students to relative autonomy. In other words we tend not to see relatively 'tutor-centred' methods, such as lecturing, as being group-based, only those methods which are more obviously 'student-centred'. Thus we may lose useful insights that could be applied to more conservative methods.

While we cannot avoid working with groups, we do have a chance to influence how well we do it. If we are to exploit group-based learning fully we need to take into account its complexity, including issues such as structure; delivery; type of material; the basics of group dynamics; extent of preparation; and extent of social interaction. Groups provide opportunities that cannot be realized through individual learning situations. They provide expertise from the rest of the group not available to the solitary individual; they can motivate and encourage; they can be used to tackle more complex and realistic tasks than on an individual basis. A group is a place where individual views of reality can be challenged and new insights obtained from debate.

What are we trying to do?

As any new educational method grows there is a tendency, good and necessary at first, to try the new method in any conceivable situation without necessarily asking why. This gives impetus and creates unanticipated successes. It builds up a valuable base of experience which can be used constructively in future design. This phase of relatively uncritical experimentation needs to be followed by careful evaluation and reflection.

In a book devoted to one particular method it is important to remind ourselves precisely why we are using it. In education it is usually enthusiasts who battle against the odds to establish new methods. We must always, however, confront enthusiasts of particular methods of learning, including ourselves, with the questions: 'Why are we using these methods?', 'Do they benefit the student?', 'Where is our evidence?' Methods should be chosen to create an environment in which students can learn effectively. They must do this within the resources and within the constraints which are defined by society and which may change with time.

One of the reasons behind the recent shift in educational methods is the change in the student population. In Sir Christopher Ball's phrase, 'more means different'. Numbers are increasing and the range of students' backgrounds is widening. We are now forced to take account of what we have previously tended to evade: that individuals learn in very different ways and their learning is different in different contexts. This means we have even more need than before to produce a varied diet of learning experiences for our students.

Influencing learning approaches and outcomes

At the same time we should also take account of the fact that our choice of teaching method ideally should be determined by the extent to which that method will facilitate learning in the particular circumstance. Learning can be defined not only as an accumulation of facts, techniques and skills but also as an internal change in the way things are understood, or in the way 'reality' is viewed. Research suggests that the outcome of learning is influenced by the intentions of the learner, and that there are two main types of approach to learning. A 'surface' approach to learning is the intention to accumulate information and factual knowledge without 'digesting' it in any way; a 'deep' approach to learning is the intention to understand and process that which is being learned, so that it will tend to result in a change in the learner's view of reality. (In Chapter 2, Tribe also considers deep and surface learning but from a slightly different viewpoint.)

Most teachers in higher education would immediately agree that it is important to encourage a deep approach to learning. Fortunately we can help to influence the student approach by providing the right kind of learning experience. The use of group-based activities can encourage a deep approach to learning to be taken through, for example, the need to debate issues.

Groups can provide a place where subject material can be fully engaged with, processed and integrated into the learner's pre-existing conception of reality. Personal responsibility to fellow students can be a motivating factor in actually getting to grips with the subject. Group-work is often an extremely effective method of achieving this deep approach. The reverse, however, can also be true: if the group dynamics cause members to withdraw and choose survival and a quick way out of conflict this in turn can encourage a surface approach to learning.

Through group-based activities interpersonal skills can also be practised and material learnt in 'real life' situations. It is possible, through careful course design, to use groups to combine both interpersonal skills and discipline-based learning. Peer feedback can be received and given in ways that are often more effective than from a tutor. Peer tutoring in groups can provide a very powerful input from those most close to the student's own learning situation.

Aims for group-based learning

Groups provide opportunities for learning in a variety of areas and from a variety of sources. It is common to distinguish between *task* and *process*, as in some of the contributions here. The aim may be to focus on learning in one or other area, or on both at once. Process includes the whole area of the individual's response to the group and the group dynamics as well as the way in which the group goes about completing the task and its participants interact in so doing. Process issues generally are much less clear and amenable to objective formulation and expression than task issues. One of the problems of working in the process area is the difficulty of expressing things which are not easily described in words. This is perhaps most obvious in the area of group dynamics. Although it is not the aim of this book to stray too far into this it is noticeable here that teaching and learning practitioners tend to be least eloquent on process issues.

The task or process model, however, does tend to oversimplify. Figure 1.1, at the end of this chapter, indicates in a bit more detail some of the types of learning aims which we may have in using groups. Using this model, we can say that students might learn something of the group dynamics and the way in which groups work; they may learn about themselves and their own personal skills in groups and they may learn something about particular subject matter. The processes of accessing these different types of learning may be very different and require different skills. Through learning about these areas comes also a more explicit possibility of learning to improve the skills inherent in each of these learning areas.

Figure 1.1 indicates that these areas of group learning can support one another or can act to detract or swamp the designed aims of the exercise. The task itself can support or detract from other aims. The diagram also indicates the importance of knowing the reasons behind using the group exercise: being sure the task is appropriate for the desired aims and producing structures and management systems which utilize the group process to best advantage in the light of the aims of the project.

Skills for employment

Group-work also prepares graduates and makes them more immediately useful to employers. The employer view is typified by Ann Allen, of ICL, when she says:

...the experience of having been part of a learning group at university can help the new entrant into employment to become part of a working team more quickly than would otherwise be the case. Quite often in the past the world of higher education did not assist integration into this team-based approach: rather, the emphasis was on individualism and competitiveness.

Group-based learning is a method of learning which is both flexible and effective in cognitive, skill and affective learning domains. Once graduates are in employment forward-looking organizations use group-based learning for knowledge transfer, for skill practice and for impacting on attitudes in a variety of ways.

Group-based methods are used in development centres, sometimes to identify and provide a facility for potential 'high fliers', more often to provide a forum for self-awareness, recognition of development needs and to gain more information to enable development plans to be put in place.

Group-work and capability

The Royal Society of Arts' Higher Education for Capability (HEC) project has promoted many innovations in teaching in higher education. The director, Professor John Stephenson, introduced the HEC conference on group-based learning in this way:

...the HEC project is to give students the opportunity to be responsible and accountable for their own learning, as individuals and in association with others, within their mainstream studies.

Those of us in the capability movement have an image of the capable person as someone who is able to take responsibility for and explain their own continuing personal, academic and professional development, whatever the circumstances.

We are wary of defining capability in precise terms, preferring to see it as an all-round human quality, an integration of knowledge, skills and personal qualities used effectively and appropriately in response to varied, familiar and unfamiliar circumstances.

The nearest we get to definitions of capability is as a series of contexts in which we might recognize the capable person. Capability is an individual's confidence in their own ability in the context in which they take effective action; explain what they are about; live and work with others; and continue to learn from experiences in a diverse and changing society.

The key word here is *confidence*. Capable people have confidence in their ability – it is not sufficient just to *have* the ability. To develop capability through higher education we must give students the experiences which will help them build that confidence in their own ability in each of those areas.

HEC supports group-based learning because it helps students develop the kind of overall capability which we seek to develop. It also promotes the development of personal and team skills and understanding of discipline-based subject matter.

Using this book

This collection represents an invaluable resource for us to use as case studies and creative prompts for our own work. Its publication is an appropriate time for us to reflect on what we have learned and on the challenges for the future. If we are to maintain quality it is also important continually to ask fundamental questions concerning our delivery methods and to monitor their appropriateness and effectiveness.

This book gives us as readers a good opportunity to review the state of the vast and complex subject of group-based learning. We hope it can be used as a jumping-off point for further progress in using learning groups and for improvement in overall quality. It includes the 'work in progress' of practising lecturers who are still actively working things out with their students in various learning situations. It contains differing views and emphases which need to be interpreted by us and adapted to our own specific environment. Such is the challenge and excitement of all teaching and learning – and especially so when the human interaction involved is heightened through group activity.

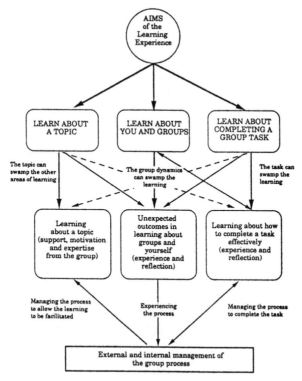

Figure 1.1 *Learning in groups: the part played by the group*

Chapter Two

An Overview from Higher Education

Diana M R Tribe

Introduction

There are two main types of purpose for group-based teaching in higher education: those related to skills acquisition and those related to academic aims.

The skills objectives of group-based learning cover such interpersonal competences as oral communication; active listening; group leadership; group membership; the ability to examine assumptions; and the ability to tolerate ambiguities. All of these skills are highly valued in employment.

The academic objectives which build on these employment skills are the ability to understand a text; question a line of argument; follow up a lecture; gauge the individual's progress on a particular course or evaluate a course.

Why use group-based learning in higher education?

Three main reasons for using group-based learning are suggested here. First, active involvement is necessary if 'real' learning is to occur. A major (and generally unquestioned) objective of higher education is to teach students to *think*, yet an examination of methods of teaching currently in use shows that students spend the majority of their working time passively receiving information and taking notes, rather than actively performing cognitive operations on the material to be learned.

Entwistle and Ramsden (1983), Marton (1976), Pask (1976) and many others have identified approaches to learning among students which may broadly be categorized into 'surface' and 'deep' processing of information. Some students (who, it would appear, tend to be less successful in examinations), take a passive approach and are mainly concerned with surface level processing of academic knowledge. Typically such students are primarily concerned with covering the content; how much they have learned; finding the 'right' answers; and assimilating unaltered pieces of knowledge (ie, those upon which they have performed no intellectual operation) by a process of rote learning. It is possible that such students have found this approach most suitable for school learning, and attempt to apply it to the higher education situation without being aware of its disadvantages.

By contrast other students, who employ deep level processing of material (and who tend to be more successful in examinations), are typically concerned with identifying the central point of an argument; what lies behind the argument; the overall picture; the logic of an argument; points that remain unclear and questioning conclusions. In short, deep processors tend to be more concerned with understanding and thinking than with assimilation, and are more versatile, finding it easier to tackle questions than do surface processors.

Research into group learning has flourished over the past few years, and has been conducted both from interactional and cognitive perspectives. The findings demonstrate that, generally, the achievements of students who work in cooperative settings are superior to those of students working in competitive and individualistic settings. However, research also indicates that where students simply *observe* the working activities of others, or listen to other students' explanations, this will prove insufficient for the learning of material. Students must be actively involved in the group process for learning to occur.

The interaction variables that have been shown to be the most effective in developing learning among group members are those of giving and receiving help, both of which show a positive relation to achievement (Moust, 1983). Students who give help by explaining difficult subject matter to their peers learn more than those who do not. The effect on achievement of receiving help depends upon that help involving an explanation as well as a correct answer.

The second major reason for using group-based learning in higher education is that a varied learning environment meets the needs of different types of students. The research into approaches to learning referred to above has implications for the teaching processes adopted in higher education. Many courses, especially those with a high lecture content and heavy pressure of examinations, are likely to inhibit (desirable) deep processing of information, and to encourage (undesirable) surface processing and rote learning. On the other hand, discussion and other activities in seminar groups are more likely to encourage deep processing of information.

For the sake of those students whose cognitive style leads them to operate a deep processing approach to learning, it is important to provide them with the academic opportunity to do so. This is best achieved, as Entwistle suggests, by providing them with the chance to learn through the operation of both large and small group methods. It is also important to demonstrate this alternative style for the sake of the surface processors, in order to give them the opportunity to model their behaviour on that of their peers. It is likely, moreover, that there are some versatile students who actually employ both surface and deep learning techniques to suit their varying needs from time to time. These students will also benefit from a learning environment which provides the opportunity for both deep and surface processing of information.

As a third major reason for using group-based learning techniques, group activities provide a sound basis for the development of the skills required for employment, such as those outlined above.

The introduction of group-based methods to higher education

There has been pressure for the last 25 years to integrate general interpersonal and group skills training within the academic content of all undergraduate degree courses in the UK. The Robbins Report identified this as a pressing need as early as 1964, yet by 1984 the University Grants Committee was still urging higher education institutions to take the problem seriously:

...the abilities most valued in industrial, commercial and professional life as well as in public and social administration are the transferable intellectual and personal skills. A higher education system which provides its students with these skills is serving society well.

Resistance to the incorporation of group-based learning into the higher education undergraduate curriculum in the UK occurred in the majority of subject areas. One reason for this resistance was the firmly entrenched view of many lecturers that such work was not appropriate to 'high level' academic study at degree level and should thus be left for students to develop at the professional stage of training or when they were eventually in employment. However, the opposing view – that the development of group skills in a higher education context does require a high level of academic rigour – is gaining ground among lecturers in the new universities (and in a few older universities) as staff increase their experience.

There has also been a fear that lecturing staff, employed for their academic subject knowledge, would not have the expertise to provide the necessary training for group-based work, even if such training were thought to be a desirable component of undergraduate education. This problem has to a certain extent been addressed through staff development programmes within institutions, though there is still much to be achieved in this sphere.

There has, however, continued to be pressure from outside bodies, as well as from intending employers (represented by the Standing Conference on Graduate Employment) to incorporate personal transferable skills development into higher education. As a result, there has been a growing trend over the past ten years for those courses which were until recently validated by the Council for National Academic Awards (that is, courses in the former polytechnics and colleges) to include training in what are variously referred to as enterprise or interpersonal skills. These are taught alongside the academic material traditionally associated with undergraduate study.

The Royal Society of Arts' Higher Education for Capability movement and the Enterprise in Higher Education movement in the UK have both encouraged and in some cases funded curriculum innovation in the teaching and assessment of skills on undergraduate programmes. So too has the CNAA, through, for example, its research into profiling and records of achievement as methods of assessing skills training programmes. Members of Her Majesty's Education Inspectorate, who as arbiters of quality became increasingly influential in the former polytechnic sector, also used their influence to encourage the development of new assessment techniques to assess the personal and interpersonal skills of students, and the greater use of more varied teaching techniques to encourage student participation.

Why *not* use group-based learning in higher education?

Several arguments are advanced against using groups. To begin with, staff and external validating bodies feel students cannot cover the syllabus fully other than by formal lectures. This argument is easily rebutted: the concept of 'full' syllabus coverage is an outdated one in the majority of curriculum areas. The advance of information and the change in subject content is so rapid that it is no longer specific content that is important but rather the research methods, forms of reasoning and logic associated with it. This is certainly the case in my own subject area (law) and it seems that this applies equally in other rapidly changing subjects. As a result total syllabus coverage ceases to be a desirable, or even a possible, aim for the majority of lecturing staff.

Further, it is argued that lecturing staff feel unhappy in a situation which is not 'teacher controlled'. This can also be rebutted. Experience of group-based methods of learning shows that whilst initially academic colleagues are wary of adopting a teaching method which they themselves did not experience as undergraduates, the pressures of increasing numbers of students without a corresponding increase in resources actually leads staff to prefer active group-based approaches to managing learning.

No longer is a member of staff the sole repository of knowledge; no longer is it her responsibility, and hers alone, to identify, explain and transmit knowledge to her students. Group activities, where properly structured, mean that students can assume some of this responsibility, to their own and their lecturers' benefit.

Another argument is that students feel unhappy in a situation which is not teacher-dependent. It is certainly true that the majority of students initially feel threatened by the introduction of new learning techniques – none more so than the surface (and often inadequate) learner. However, in practice most students are quick to see the advantages of group learning methods and will adapt relatively rapidly to a change of approach. Of course there will always be some students who prefer the standard lecture and a 'good set of notes', and such students will no doubt be voluble in their complaints at a change in style. Remember, however, that the old technique of knowledge transmission via dictated lecture notes was only ever appropriate for at best a half of the students (the rote learners) and that for the deep processors a more active and participative style is certainly more likely to inculcate knowledge.

Finally, it is claimed that lecturing staff feel they do not have the necessary skills to set up group-based learning activities. This is certainly a problem for staff who are set in their ways; however, there is now available a wide range of materials to help staff develop new techniques (for example, HERDSA Green Guides, and the '53 Interesting Ways to Teach' series by Gibbs *et al.*). Although funds for staff development are no doubt increasingly scarce, there is no reason why interested groups of staff cannot set up their own discussion groups to develop new techniques on the basis of some of the published materials.

Curriculum implications

Staff time and resources for staff development need to be made available at the outset of any curriculum change, and this is certainly the case where group-based learning is initiated. However, the eventual saving of time and effort for the staff involved and the enthusiasm and success of the students more than compensate for any initial outlay in setting up the system.

Fundamental to this approach is the development of materials which both explain the new arrangements in a way which ensures that staff and students understand the reasons for change and how they will be affected by it, and provide structured materials as a basis for group activity. Nothing is more likely to ensure failure than the lack of clear structured exercises for students to carry out, and the absence of an accompanying lecturers' handbook.

The development of appropriate assessment mechanisms is essential. Considerable expertise has already been gained in relation to new forms of assessment for group-based learning activities. The CNAA, prior to its demise, funded several research projects into alternative methods of assessment in a variety of curriculum areas. In law, for example, this has resulted in assessment of group activities such as mock trials and interviewing and negotiating tasks, group presentations and group reports, all now contributing towards final degree classification in many universities.

The CNAA profiling project, which investigated the development of student records of achievement, has been particularly helpful in this context. Clearly, different curriculum areas will require the development of different skills and different methods of assessment, and this will be a task for the subject specialists and the professional bodies involved.

The views of the external professional bodies are often cited as a reason for 'full' syllabus coverage which, it is alleged, necessarily militates against the adoption of group-based methods of working. However, Higher Education for Capability colloquia held recently to explore the views of the professional bodies (in, for example, accounting, engineering, computer science and law), showed plainly that the professional bodies are very much in favour of developing in students those skills which are acquired through group learning activities.

Many professional bodies which validate undergraduate courses now specifically require the incorporation of group-based activities into the curriculum. These bodies are only too well aware that the competitive individualistic graduate who finds it difficult to work cooperatively with their work colleagues is not therefore a desirable entrant to a profession.

References

Entwistle, N and Ramsden, P (1983) *Understanding Student Learning,* Beckenham: Croom Helm.

Gibbs, G *et al* (1984 – to date) *53 Interesting Ways to Teach* Series, Bristol: Technical and Educational Services.

HERDSA (1984 – to date) *Green Guide* Series, Kensington, NSW: Higher Education Research and Development Society for Australasia.

Marton, P (1976) 'On qualitative differences in learning' *British Journal of Educational Psychology*, 46, 1 and 2.

Moust, H C *et al.* (1983) 'Effects of verbal participation in group discussion' *Student Learning: Research in Education & Cognitive Psychology*, OU/SRHE.

Pask, K (1976) 'Styles and strategies of learning' *British Journal of Educational Psychology*, 46, 2.

Part Two: The Experience

Learning Group Skills

This section concentrates on the earliest stages of group-based learning, describing ways in which students can be introduced to the experience and ways in which staff themselves may begin.

To be able to learn effectively in a group setting participants must first be able to cope within the group's complex interpersonal environment. Despite the fact that we have all been existing in a variety of groups since earliest childhood, it would be wrong to assume that we all automatically possess the necessary skills to function effectively.

Learning groups are distinct from other types of group. They require special skills. Most of us acquire these skills only gradually and often with difficulty. Students who are plunged into group learning without adequate assistance in managing the group processes may do well – but all too often they find the group learning experience negative. This may not only reduce learning at the time but also possibly on future occasions.

The recognition that students need some kind of preparation for group-work is thus gaining ground. However, experience suggests that student motivation for input on group skills is often low as the students themselves do not usually recognize the need for it. To provide motivation the input must be presented so as to be seen as either obviously relevant to the curriculum or as meeting the students' own perceived needs in some way.

Both these tactics are used by Garland in the UPshot Programme at the University of Plymouth. This programme involves all first-year students from a large degree course during their induction period. It answers the perceived needs of the students in that it helps them to become familiar with their new environment and to make new relationships with each other at the same time as it introduces them to working in groups.

Student motivation is also likely to be increased by the fact that their work will be built on in the organizational behaviour module which follows.

Robson of the University of Luton describes practical exercises aimed at transforming a 'nominal group into a cohesive unit'. Group-forming activities such as those discussed here can be highly motivating and crucial in helping a group relax, but Robson properly sounds some notes of caution. Icebreakers and other exercises aimed at 'getting groups going' need to be used with care, with tutor skill and with acceptance of the fact that there are significant individual differences in the way in which participants learn to become effective members of groups. While the process of learning to work in a group is very necessary, some participants can find such exercises stressful or even threatening and prefer more structured learning events with early concentration on relevant tasks.

The chapter by Newman and Nelder at Cranfield University sets in context the way group projects are used in a postgraduate course. Students are given the opportunity to acquire team-work skills through small exercises and a large self-managed project. Motivation is ensured by the discipline-orientated project and by the presence of an industrial sponsor who is a 'customer to be satisfied'. Newman and Nelder also give an insight into the complexity of group project self-management.

Changing from an emphasis on 'teaching' to an emphasis on 'learning' will usually result in increased student collaboration, so that peers can support one another as they seek to achieve greater independence in their studies. Guzkowska and Kent of University College London have introduced team-work and leadership into an innovative personal development programme for students from across the college. The participation of employers again adds an important element of credibility to an area where students will often question its relevance to their studies.

In the final chapter in this section, Rawlinson at the University of Surrey describes a specialized technique, called synectics, which can be used with groups with the aim of freeing members to participate creatively. The surprisingly low emphasis on the development of creativity in higher education, whether through team-work or otherwise, makes this technique especially welcome.

Chapter Three

The UPshot Programme: Improving Group-work Skills for Business and Accounting Students

Diane Garland

The UPshot programme

UPshot is an innovative programme designed to introduce group-work skills to first-year business and accounting degree students; it forms part of the business skills programme at the University of Plymouth.

The aims of the UPshot programme are to introduce students to the ways in which groups work; to develop knowledge of the university campus and city; and to widen the students' circle of friends at the start of the course. A total of 350 students, working in groups of six (some groups including students from up to four different degree courses) participated in the first UPshot programme in 1992.

UPshot 1992

At the initial meeting in induction week the students were asked to divide into groups of six and to choose a leader. Each group member was given different tasks. They were then asked to meet the following day, when they would take part in a time-constrained group-work exercise.

During the main three-hour exercise groups were required to complete several tasks. Each group needed to collect information and equipment from a variety of points in the university. They then had to collect and solve cryptic clues; obtain and use maps of the campus and city; collect and follow written instructions; take ten photographs of the campus and/or city using a polaroid camera; and finally, select three of the ten photographs to submit as the most effective and appropriate illustrations for insertion in the university prospectus.

Students were also expected to keep a team 'log'. This was to include information such as the key decisions taken, by whom, the problems encountered and interesting events. At the end of the exercise, students were required to complete individually a group behaviour questionnaire to help in analysing the effectiveness of individual and group performance. The students were also given reading material containing an overview of major theories relating to working in groups.

During the following three weeks, each group reconvened and planned a short video presentation summarizing the exercise. They were also asked to use the team log, group behaviour questionnaires and further reading material to help them draw conclusions as to how effectively the group worked. Groups then prepared and made the videos, which were intended to be as innovative and creative as possible. Debriefing sessions were held to review the programme and the learning gained. The videos were available for viewing during these sessions.

The photographs were judged by the dean of the business school and a representative of the university's marketing department. Prizes were awarded to the winning groups. Some of the photographs were used for the next university prospectus.

All 59 groups completed the first UPshot programme. Feedback from the students was positive, with students suggesting that the programme should continue to be run on similar lines. The individually completed group behaviour questionnaires, team discussions, the reading material supplied and the team log were all identified as being important in helping students to learn about working in groups.

Further work

In view of its success in providing an interesting and innovative approach to introducing group-work skills to a large number of undergraduates, UPshot will be retained as part of the course for future cohorts.

All students involved in the UPshot programme subsequently take the organizational behaviour module. Starting at the beginning of the spring term, this module features a complementary programme of lectures and videos called 'Effective Group Working', which provides theoretical input on working in groups. Students are also given individual copies of a specially prepared group-work skills manual containing back-up material and further exercises (Garland, 1992). This module thus builds on the group-work experience gained under UPshot.

Reference

Garland, D Y (1992) *Working in Groups Skills Manual,* University of Plymouth.

Chapter Four

Facilitating the Formation of Effective and Creative Working Groups

John Robson

Introduction

Group-based exercises depend upon the formation of groups within which the participants feel willing and able to contribute. The group formation process itself often receives little attention, even though numerous observers have noted how ineffective many groups can be. Before any effective group-work can occur some effort needs to be made to transform a nominal group into a cohesive unit. There is, however, often very limited time available on-course so that it is necessary to bring the people concerned up to a working level as quickly as possible.

This chapter looks at a variety of tasks which have been used as 'ice-breaking' or introductory exercises for short residential courses and in induction programmes for full-time undergraduates. The joint aims behind their use are to provide some initial skills in group learning and to help students form relationships to support each other in the early stages of their courses.

Cumulative introductions

All participants in the group, including the facilitator, sit in an informal circle. The facilitator describes the exercise (as below) and indicates that not only will he start the exercise but he will also take on the last (and most difficult) turn. The facilitator gives his name and adds something reasonably colourful about himself. The person to the left of the facilitator then repeats the facilitator's introduction and adds his own name, says something about himself, and so on. This continues until the circle is completed, with the facilitator hopefully being able to recount the names and something about each person.

Important ground rules are: no discussion of 'work' or anticipated tasks; no indication of rank or status; no discussion of courses or qualifications; names should be used accurately, and corrected by other participants if errors occur in recall.

This is a very effective exercise in that everyone learns at least most of the names very quickly. Some corruption or errors in descriptions as things progress may be a positive advantage.

The exercise is more participative than it first appears. When anyone in the group hesitates the rest of the group tend to join in. There is also much greater eye contact between participants than occurs in most early encounters; added to a certain amount of humour and an inability to carry out the task accurately this establishes the humanity of the participants and builds a level of trust and openness between the group members. This method also avoids inputs which might lead to status assumptions by members of the group about each other: this is important in the early stages of group formation.

Exercises based on seeking a consensus

Participants are given a list of ten to 20 items and are asked to spend five to ten minutes working individually at ranking the items for some agreed purpose. They then come together for 20 to 30 minutes to establish a group ranking, the aim being to learn from each other and develop an overall consensus rather than to defend their own initial lists.

There are some well-known commercially produced exercises of this form (including, for example, 'survival' exercises) but it is often more productive to design one which relates to the interests of the particular group. One of the secrets is to include in the list at least one item which individual participants might be expected to view differently from each other, either because of their personal values or because it is the sort of item about which people assume an expertise that they do not possess. One word of warning: avoid emotive items. The aim of the exercise is to bring groups together.

This type of exercise gets people working together and can be a useful vehicle for developing factual content. Such exercises can be used to illustrate points on time-management; to demonstrate the way most groups consider task needs rather than group needs; and to encourage discussion on aspects of group dynamics and group effectiveness. Any behaviour changes necessary to enhance group effectiveness that are recognized in this way will usually be implemented by the group, thus making it more effective in subsequent work.

Problems based on arithmetic and logic

This type of exercise is generally based on an apparently well-defined problem which is subject to minor difficulties of interpretation. Usually it includes a set of straightforward but confusing and possibly irrelevant transactions. The group will probably fail, at least initially, to distinguish between solutions which are fundamentally different (thus implying one of them to be in error) and solutions which if explained or thought through sufficiently carefully are found to be equivalent.

Such exercises often begin with participants working in small sub-groups of about four to six and are then followed by a second phase where two or more sub-groups with different initial solutions attempt to come to an agreement.

If well designed this type of exercise has an almost compulsive appeal which is useful in generating conversation and building relationships within the group. Participants are often amazed that disagreements occur and are further surprised at both their own inability to convince others and/or the inability of others to understand.

Typical responses can also help to illustrate how difficult it is to sustain a logical argument unless it is very clearly thought out first; and that even if an argument is logical and complete it does not follow that the rest of the group will either understand or be convinced by it. Further, the exercise may well demonstrate that once a sub-group reaches consensus then 'group-think' sets in: the sub-group may well unreasonably defend its own solution against the ideas of others. Further, a sub-group will often apply sanctions against any member converted to another sub-group's position. Groups may be surprised to find that even in relation to an obviously logical problem the dominant modes of interaction are political rather than rational.

Finally, attention can be drawn to the fact that group-work is not the ideal mode for all problems: as here, problems are often best solved by an individual working alone. It should be recognizable to the group that they would be more effective if they delegated the task to one member and then received and verified the results.

Problems involving explanations of physical behaviour

Here the facilitator introduces a problem that appears simple but cannot easily be explained in terms of the theoretical constructs that the participants bring with them. An example is to ask participants to describe the behaviour of a plane (ie ordinary) mirror. It is predictable that someone will say that it 'laterally inverts', and when asked to expand this description that it inverts left and right but not top and bottom. But how does the mirror know which way is up?

There is a wide range of problems of this type, including many involving optics and mechanics. The best are accessible both to those who have some knowledge of elementary physics and to those who have not. Indeed, although a little knowledge of physics may help in describing the problems, it may well be insufficient for its solution: difficulties are generally caused by inadequate or inaccurate concepts (does a mirror really 'laterally invert'?).

This type of exercise is at first sight very similar to those of the previous type, but there are some significant differences in terms of group reaction. The first is that while this type of problem exhibits the same sort of compulsive fascination for some participants, others display no interest whatsoever. These problems are useful only with participants who have some interest in scientific enquiry. Second, that this is a type of problem with which groups typically perform better than individuals. Although this would seem to be a logical/analytic task at first sight, it is possible that groups perform better than individuals here because the brainstorming which occurs helps the group avoid the pitfalls of being trapped in conventional thought patterns.

Ineffective strategies

Finally, some observations on strategies which appear to be ineffective in helping to develop a working group.

First, going round a group asking people to introduce themselves and say what they do will not help. Very little is remembered, possibly because no one is interested or involved. It can also cause embarrassment. Second, using psychometric testing as a means of selecting groups, assuming that if the group is put together carefully then a separate stage of group building will not be needed, does not work. The group will still need to go through a developmental stage in order to be effective. Third, using a presentation as initial input before moving on to the actual group-work is ineffective. This approach may enhance task skills but in many groups these are not in short supply. In most group-work what are really needed are the process or group skills. These are most effectively developed in the group context itself.

Conclusion

The exercises described above are simply a limited subset of tasks which are currently being used in a variety of institutions to get groups working together.

All the exercises discussed are open to criticism in that they can be perceived as taking up time which might be better used for substantive content, yet group building can be seen as an essential phase through which a group must go in order to become effective. Developing this openly and consciously will save time rather than add to the total. In many cases a usefully performing group can be developed in as little as one to two hours.

Acknowledgements: to John Martin, Victor Bignell and Tony Wright of the Open University.

Chapter Five

Towards Self-managed Projects: Learning Team Techniques

Victor Newman and Geoff Nelder

Introduction

The use of team-work in industry is growing as the benefits are recognized and as examples of success through team-work proliferate. Employers increasingly seek evidence of team-work skills alongside technical competence in their new recruits. In response to this the CIM Institute at Cranfield University has focused on team-work as a central, integral part of the overall learning environment for its MSc students.

The taught programme for the course delivers knowledge of concepts, theory and examples of team-work. The students then acquire and practice team-work skills through a number of practical minor projects. Finally, the students undertake a commercial, self-managed group project which further develops their understanding of team-working and in which their ability to learn, work and deliver as a team is the key factor for success.

The taught programme contributes 25 per cent of the total MSc programme, the group project 35 per cent and an individual project 40 per cent. This emphasis on project-based learning prepares students for continuous learning throughout their careers.

Self-managed group projects

Each student is assigned to a commercial group project as part of a team of normally six to 12 students. An academic tutor/supervisor is allocated to each project. The nominal project objective is different for each team, but all teams will share a similar learning experience. The purpose of its being a group project is to develop in students the knowledge of how teams work, the skills required to perform in a team and the understanding which comes from observing and reflecting on their own experience. This leads to learning points which they can apply in future.

The commercial sponsor is invaluable in providing an interface with the rigours and demands of the 'real world' and, by commitment, proving that the project is worthwhile and that there is a demand for the project outcomes. This becomes a powerful motivating factor for the students. The sponsor adds a dimension to the project that could not adequately be provided in a purely academic environment.

For the team, managing the relationship with the sponsor becomes a significant overhead. To be successful, they must identify an agreed customer, a representative of the sponsor who can speak for all the sponsor's interests; they must agree and if necessary refine the initial proposal in terms of outputs, approach, scope and timing; they must put in place lines of communication; and agree a system for reporting progress. They must also recognize that the sponsor's interests are likely to change during the course of the project. As interim results become available, so the team must allow flexibility and agree the limits of that flexibility.

The tutor prepares the initial proposal with the sponsor so that the project team can be given a clear start point. With the team, the tutor helps in the creation of a working environment and in establishing behavioural systems which enable individual and team development. Part of this process includes negotiation of assessment criteria.

The tutor is not the project leader or manager: these responsibilities are assumed by the team. During the project, the tutor attends regular progress meetings and, where appropriate, will offer advice on process and identify learning points. The tutor's role is to help the students to understand and learn from the experience of undertaking a team-based project.

Although it is desirable for the team to take full responsibility for managing their interaction with the sponsor there are circumstances where this may not be feasible. There may be political considerations internal to the sponsor company or which affect the sponsor's relationship with the university; these will require the tutor's attention. Other difficulties can arise if the project is educationally successful, in that the learning content is high, but it is not meeting its commercial objectives. In these situations the tutor must act as gatekeeper, allowing the team some interaction with the sponsor, while controlling harmful interactions to preserve learning opportunities.

At the end of the project, the tutor should assume responsibility for continued liaison with the sponsor, and assess and debrief the students.

Factors for success

After an initial briefing, the project team is faced with the problem of how to proceed from their current position to one in which, in 14 weeks time, they will be able to deliver acceptable project outputs to the sponsor.

Experience has shown that, in order to ensure eventual success, the team must take care of a number of *project management* tasks and issues. The team must satisfy itself that it has a clear specification and an identified customer, and that the team and customer agree on interpretation of the specification, work to be done and project outputs. The team members must establish a relationship with their customer including channels of communication; formal reporting procedures for access to customer sites and personnel; agreed levels of demand for customer resources (staff-time, use of equipment, consumption of materials, expenses budgets); and matters such as on-site dress codes and behaviour.

The group must develop a clear idea of the central problem or issue in order to keep sight of its primary purpose: group members should prepare a mission statement encapsulating the problem and detailing specific tasks. A project plan to determine when each identified task is to be performed and what resources are required will also be needed.

As work proceeds, several tasks will be running concurrently and each team member is likely to be allocated more than one task. It is in the team's own interest to spread workloads by allocating task leaderships across all individuals. A central management function must be designed in order to coordinate this.

Project management should involve the whole team at formal meetings. This ensures that all work done is reported, that the whole team is aware of progress, and it contributes to individual motivation as a visible record of achievement. The formal meeting also serves academic purposes, gives an opportunity for the tutor to encourage reflection on the project and learning processes, and the project objectives, and provides a contemporaneous project record which is valuable later in project assessment.

Established standards are needed for a variety of progress reports. These may range from verbal reports to the formal meeting recorded in minutes, to documentation presented to the formal meeting and reports prepared for the sponsor. These will form part of the project record and contribute to the project assessment and project audit if required. The team can measure its own performance against the project specification using the mechanisms of the project plan. The tutor's judgement on the team's performance will also be useful: the team should seek tutor feedback and design a feedback mechanism.

The project specification defines what is to be delivered by the team. Typical project outputs include an academic project report; a customer report; a formal presentation of results; a working demonstrator system; a software product; technical handbooks; and training workshops. A delivery process must be designed by the team for each identified output, with the tasks created becoming part of the overall project activity.

The factors from specification through to delivery determine the methodology that will be used to undertake the project. Testing this methodology on a small scale as part of the planning phase provides learning opportunities, allows the methodology to be fine-tuned and builds confidence. Finally, the team should ensure that the project finishes tidily after the project outputs have been transferred to the customer.

Conclusion

Experience of working in a team is, in itself, of only limited benefit. To benefit fully from curriculum-based team-working the student must be involved in the development of the team-work and team-management process, must take part in that process as a member and leader, and must have opportunities to reflect on the performance of the process as well as the project outcomes. The CIM Institute has developed and implemented learning team techniques to meet these requirements and to equip its students with transferable team-work skills.

Chapter Six

Facilitating Team-work in the Curriculum

Myszka Guzkowska and Ivan Kent

Introduction

'Much learning does not teach understanding' wrote Heraclitus. It is a measure of the enormous inertia of educational institutions that, despite pressure to change, the majority of undergraduates are still being *taught* rather than *encouraged to learn*. Initiatives such as the Employment Department's Enterprise in Higher Education (EHE) programme and the Royal Society of Arts' Higher Education for Capability (HEC) project are proof of the effort needed to overcome such inertia.

This chapter is concerned with one aspect of the management of change at University College London (UCL): changing the ways in which learning is facilitated in a fairly traditional university. Specifically, it looks at how students can be encouraged and supported in developing the skills which facilitate their learning abilities and better prepare them for whatever career they may pursue after graduation.

Origins of the personal development programme

In 1989 UCL initiated a programme intended to equip undergraduates with a range of personal transferable skills which would be useful to them both during their university studies and thereafter. At the time, both the EHE programme and the HEC project were raising awareness of the need for change in higher education. It was decided that, in line with their interests, UCL would pilot a programme focusing on team-work, leadership, communication and project management skills. The resulting personal development programme (PDP) was designed to be college-wide, to work in collaboration with employers and to act as a 'seed' activity from which experience could be gained and cascaded down the departmental structure in order, eventually, to embed these skills in the curriculum.

Course design

In designing the programme there were three objectives. First, it had to develop an individual's skills – whatever their initial level of experience. Second, it had to have immediate practical benefits for the participants and, third, it had to be capable of being built into academic curricula.

The first objective was met by adopting an experiential ethos. Drawing on Kolb's model of experiential learning (Kolb, 1984), the participants' development would be facilitated by using practical exercises followed by reviews, action planning, reflection and subsequent reapplication. This would allow students to build on their existing skills and, through the review process, to share their learning with others in the group.

The second objective was to be achieved through a focus on personal transferable skills, specifically team-work, leadership, communication and project management skills. Not only were these skills which, it was perceived, employers valued but they could be put together in a way which employed the synergistic dynamic of the experiential learning cycle. In this process each new skill worked on adds to the value of application of the skills which precede it.

The third objective was to be met by encouraging the members of staff involved to themselves participate in the experiential learning experience. Many lecturers were known to favour a more facilitative role and, in theory, supported the idea of students becoming self-managed learners. For reasons as diverse as cynicism and departmental tradition, however, teaching staff were generally reluctant to change their methods without some indication that the effort might be worth it. In order to achieve the third objective it was realized that the staff would have to learn from their students that these skills could be applied in an academic situation.

Core skills

In looking at the structure of a course it was decided to take an holistic approach: though modular, the course was to involve (for practical and theoretical reasons) a continuous process rather than a sequential series of independent events. Because groups are to be found in social, learning and work situations the underlying theme of the course was to be group-work.

Group-work skills would be applied in a variety of situations designed to illuminate the dynamics of a group and the roles individuals take, including aspects such as problem solving; planning; communication; the functions of leadership; and the organization of information, material and people in order to achieve specific tasks.

A series of core skills were identified, each of which would be intro-duced and then developed through a series of activities. Each activity would have a specific focus and each would also utilize all the learning gained from earlier exercises and develop it further. The pilot course included:

- *Introduction to team-work* – intended as an opportunity for participants to develop their understanding of group processes and the elements of leadership through a series of exercises and reviews.
- *Team-work and leadership* – designed to develop further the understand-ing of group processes, planning and communication through a chal-lenging series of practical, team-based exercises offering leadership opportunities to all participants, including reviews, reflection and action planning.
- *Communication skills* – intended to develop communication skills in a variety of situations, through video-recorded oral presentation skills training with group feedback and team role plays, in a variety of com-munication settings and including reviews and action planning.
- *Project management* – designed to develop an understanding of the processes of managing a project by means of a number of exercises, covering individual time-management and project-management skills, concluding with a complex competitive team exercise involving all the preceding skills.

From the outset the intention was to seek partnership with interested employers. Employer involvement, through the use of their staff and their premises, was expected to provide added value for participants by extending their knowledge of the range of employment opportunities and providing a practical insight into the working environment. Touche Ross and Coopers and Lybrand agreed to support the programme. The 'Introduction to Team-work' element was to be run by the authors at UCL and the 'Team-work and Leadership' element by them with the support of a management training company, Trojan Training Limited.

The personal development programme

The first PDP recruited 30 second-year students, representing 21 different departments and all seven faculties for the pilot programme. Beginning in

October 1990, it comprised nine days over four weekends in the autumn and spring terms.

Assessment was formative and by facilitated peer review during the group review sessions. At the end of the course the facilitators wrote open references for each of the participants. The reference served a dual purpose: first, it formed the basis for discussion at a final course interview in which performance was reviewed; and second, it was available to the student to use in support of subsequent applications for employment or further education. Participants stated that they found the reference and interview useful because, as well as having the practical benefit of supporting job applications, it summarized the outcome of the programme and helped them put the experience into a wider context.

Outcomes

Specific outcomes for individual participants are difficult to judge objectively because there is no way of referencing the actual outcome with what might have been, had there been no PDP course. Subjectively, participants reported an increase in self-confidence, particularly with regard to oral presentations and in negotiations of various kinds. Some participants stated that PDP had helped them to make decisions they might not otherwise have made (course changes, career decisions and so on) and several said they had become more confident in making decisions than they felt they otherwise would have been. In at least three cases PDP appears to have helped participants target, and get, the jobs they particularly wanted against strong competition.

It is possible to be more objective about the institutional outcomes. PDP was an instrumental factor in preparing the way for, and gaining, a contract from the Department of Employment in the fourth round of the EHE initiative, beginning in July 1991. Feedback from several departments noted that students who had been on PDP were noticeably more confident and more willing to engage in departmental level activities, such as committees. As a result it has aided the credibility of, and enthusiasm for, similar activities as part of the EHE programme.

Participants expressed a desire to continue their involvement with PDP. This resulted in two ex-PDP students volunteering to serve as student representatives on the enterprise board, the formation of a student enterprise society and eight students from the first year of the PDP programme returning to act as facilitators during its second year. This proved to be so successful it has led to student facilitators becoming a permanent feature of the course.

Conclusion

At the time of writing, PDP is in its third year, with 100 student participants plus 32 student facilitators drawn from the previous year's participants. In addition to being instrumental in gaining Department of Employment EHE funding, PDP has built up a store of experience in core skills development which is vital to the development of departmental initiatives. A range of training events (team-work, leadership, communication and interview skills) have been run in departments for students and for staff.

Some departments have used PDP students to assist in departmental activities, while the student enterprise society has begun to develop its own activities both within UCL and as part of the southern region and national student enterprise networks. In one department, an ex-PDP student personally initiated a team-building weekend for newly arrived first-year students. This was so successful that the weekend will be continued in future years.

Because PDP is based on group-work and as it extends right across UCL, it has proved to be a vital mechanism in demonstrating the practical benefits of, and encouraging departmental interest in, group-based learning activities. The departments of chemical and biochemical engineering, Italian, geology, geography and anatomy and developmental biology have all begun to embed team-based experiential activities into their curricula.

Acknowledgements: the support given to PDP by the Employment Department, Touche Ross, Coopers and Lybrand, Procter and Gamble Limited, IBM, the Army and KPMG is gratefully acknowledged.

Reference

Kolb, D A (1984) *Experiential Learning*, New York: Prentice-Hall.

Chapter Seven

Synectics in Higher Education
Graham Rawlinson

Background

Synectics UK Ltd is a consultancy company delivering innovation in top UK companies. The processes developed result from active research into innovation, via examination of how people working in teams communicate and solve problems. A key element of the research is the use of video to review what people actually do and how their behaviour helps or hinders solution finding. The processes developed are based on experience rather than theory and the courses and consultancy offered are centred on improving people's skills in managing team-work, problem solving and communication (Hicks, 1991; Nolan, 1989).

These developments stem from the originators of Synectics in the USA, leading to a world-wide commercial organization, in which Synectics is embedded into major companies. Some of these have used Synectics processes consistently for more than 20 years and report large financial savings.

Synectics in education

Over the last few years, Synectics UK has supported the development of Synectics processes in education. Some Local Education Authorities are delivering Synectics courses to all senior and junior managers. This has led to the setting up of the Synectics Education Initiative, with the purpose of delivering Synectics processes throughout the education system. Annual conferences are now held in Britain.

In higher education, the Synectics Innovative Team-Work Programme (ITP) is the central method of introducing Synectics processes. The ITP is a three-day course originally developed for Exxon plc, designed specifically to introduce people to Synectics processes and to develop the skills of participants. The programme has been run as a staff course at four higher education institutions so far, with several others planned. It has been seen as valuable for resource managers, counsellors, staff developers and general course teachers.

The ITP covers key areas of communication in teams: the help or hindrance value of questions; how to offer, accept and build on ideas; how to develop ideas openly as 'springboards' and then focus slowly towards solutions. The programme outlines the key role of the problem owner; the functioning of the effective facilitator; and the use of the team as a resource for new ideas. The programme develops techniques for creative connection-making to generate new ideas; shows participants how to listen for ideas rather than listen for understanding; and the power of suspending judgement. The ITP also introduces the Synectics agenda meeting as an efficient and effective way of running meetings.

Synectics processes aid management and decision making. They can be used to help develop student self-managed learning and generally can be used as a teaching process. The Synectics processes are of proven value when new solutions are needed, when conflicts need resolution (as a mediation process) and to aid unravelling of complex processes.

Programmes are now being run to produce more Synectics accredited trainers to work in education. Accredited trainers are free to deliver courses under licence in their own institutions and, within the Synectics Education Initiative, to other institutions. The future of the Synectics Education Initiative will follow the wishes of its members, seeking new inventions and methods of developing delivery methods to meet local needs.

The Enterprise in Higher Education Initiative sets out to develop personal transferable skills of students, often via innovations in teaching processes: the Synectics course is of proven value in this field. The course is valuable for skills development for both staff and students. Courses run with a combined group of staff and students have been especially effective and endorse the concept of partnership between students and staff.

Synectics at the University of Surrey

The ITP is currently being integrated into an undergraduate engineering course at the University of Surrey. With funding from Pegasus, a charity supporting innovation in teaching in higher education, staff at Surrey have re-written the ITP as 'Creative Problem Solving in Teams' so that academic staff could deliver key parts of the course to students within a two-day period.

A *Participants' Manual* of some 60 pages has been written in open learning style, so that students can use the manual later for further exercises as well as for helping them understand what happens. The result is a great success, with staff pleased that they can switch from teaching to facilitating and impressed with the impact that this makes on students working in teams on a major design project. It is intended that the manual can be taken up by course directors in other areas: it has been made as transferable as possible so that it can be used with minimum change and maximum flexibility.

A member of academic staff reports that, as a result of Synectics, 'students are asking fundamental questions whereas previously they asked the obvious. They are much further on in design issues. The whole department is now behind this approach to team-work'. These encouraging results have led us to make the student course available to other universities.

References

Hicks, M J (1991) *Problem Solving in Business and Management: Hard, soft and creative processes,* London: Chapman and Hall.

Nolan, V (1989) *The Innovators Handbook,* London: Sphere Books.

Section Two:

Managing Group Learning

The chapters in this section recognize that in addition to preparing the students for group-work, the staff need to be prepared too. Many academic staff have spent only a small amount of their working time in groups and probably even less of their own educational time. Those with little recent industrial experience, therefore, may have little expertise in group-work. In using group-work they will, in addition, have to change roles from being a 'centre stage' lecturer to becoming a 'facilitator' working together with the students.

There are also greater demands to produce clear and effective written materials for staff working with independent project groups than for staff working in closer contact with students. To ensure that effective learning takes place, the group process needs careful management. Group management needs to be 'light' enough to allow students to learn for themselves, but with sufficient 'steerage' for students to feel they are achieving something and to ensure that the group process does not swamp the learning (see Figure 1.1, at the end of Chapter 1). This is the art of the lecturer turned facilitator.

Stone of the Manchester Metropolitan University gives a useful overview of the careful preparation necessary for managing group projects, illustrating the care needed in setting up a new project. The assessment procedure used is a helpful attempt at letting the students be part of the assessment process.

Gregory and Thorley, at the University of Hertfordshire, have addressed the issue of staff development for supervisors by providing a four-day residential course. The course involves the staff in themselves experiencing task-related group exercises in order to help them understand the way groups work and how students feel when put in similar situations. From this the tutors are encouraged to reassess their own design and management of group learning processes.

Dawson, Lord and Baggott of Thames Valley University have designed an interesting study on the effect of group composition on the students' perceptions of their own learning. The question of group composition is often asked by practitioners but rarely addressed in the literature. When the final results of this study are known, further work in this area will still be needed in order to ensure that students have positive experiences in groups and that we continually question the effectiveness of their use.

Experience gained at the University of Teesside on a DMS project enables Mathews to give a detailed account of the way peer assessment can be used in groups. The system has been successfully used for a part of the final assessment and could be a useful model to adapt to other situations.

Chapter Eight

The Academic Management of Group Projects

Brian Stone

Introduction

Her Majesty's Inspectors' reports on higher education had at least the salutary effect of causing course management teams to examine themselves for management rigour as well as for academic respectability. HMI used four headings under which they assessed performance and sought excellence: *context, content, process* and *outcome*. Central to all these is *management*.

This chapter examines the role and functions of the academic manager in group projects and looks at elements of good practice in three of these four areas. It cannot, of course, address *context*, as this is discipline-based.

The objectives of group projects

The first act when setting up a group project should be to set educational objectives. Like everything else these are subject to management: groundwork here is essential, especially as objectives set the *context* of the managed event.

People are goal-oriented and will point themselves and their efforts towards objectives. In order to be constructive in group project design terms, the objectives should be relevant to the academic achiever; attainable, not obviously beyond reach; but also challenging and not too easy; clear, visible and repeatedly indicated; agreed rather than imposed unilaterally; and rewarded, though not in this case in material terms.

Objectives can be defined as 'what we are supposed to achieve'. Group project-based work ought to be characterized by objectives that are set and agreed in advance and its success measurable by the extent to which these objectives are achieved. The danger lies in fixing the intentions on merely 'what we are supposed to *complete*', which implies being satisfied with an acceptable level of work instead of a high standard. This trap can be particularly tempting if the project work is client-based, in that academics can bias the project towards efforts to satisfy clients through their own need for 'repeat business', thus compromising academic standards.

The objectives must also be translated into practical terms. There are four key steps:

- to set and agree academic objectives with students and, if appropriate, to agree key result areas with clients;
- to agree specific objectives within the group project, including deadlines;
- to allocate and agree targets with group members;
- to publish the finalized objectives to all concerned (managers, tutors, administrators, students, clients, *et al.*) so that there is a point of final reference in case of dispute, and so that there is a core for debate of overall issues at the outset, during progress, and in review.

Performance criteria

In the academic context it is usual to grade performance by degree division, often including a numerical mark, or in BTEC cases to assign a grading. In group project work this is likely to involve sophisticated academic judgement. A clear written specification of what constitutes an appropriate standard of performance to obtain a grade in each division would be useful. But when asked to specify, for example, what characterizes a first-class honours performance, academics tend to assert their ability to 'know one when they see one'.

It is both possible and useful, however, to draw a broad sketch of standards of performance per division and to specify that in writing. In business studies at the Manchester Metropolitan University we use the following specifications; while they can be applied to degree work in general they are phrased here so as to apply to the tangible outcomes produced in the course of project work:

First/Distinction: *extraordinary* standard of work: objectives surpassed, competence developed to excellence; high levels of intellectual rigour; complete coverage of field; excellence in care and presentation of material; innovative, ingenious or creative thinking and communication devices.

2.i/High Merit: *competent* work: objectives achieved, competence demonstrated; sound levels of intellectual rigour; entirely sufficient coverage of field; care taken in presentation; diligent thinking, sound and practical and/or interesting communication.

2.ii/Low merit: *adequate* work: objectives largely achieved, some competence demonstrated but with areas needing improvement; sufficient coverage of field; presentation adequate; evidence of some sound thinking, communication reasonably successful but capable of more clarity or impact.

3rd/Pass: *just sufficient* work: some but not all objectives achieved; bare minimum of competence and application of knowledge; field partially covered; presentation just worthy of a pass; discernible evidence of some thought; communication sufficient but poor. Just enough care taken.

Fail/Refer: *inadequate* work: few if any objectives achieved; incompetent in application of knowledge, and/or planning and conduct of the project. Field inadequately covered. Work presented with little or no care and attention; little thought evident; a failure to communicate.

These can be further modified so as to be relevant to the precise areas to be assessed, be they reports, presentations, *viva voce* examinations, exhibitions, videotapes, sound-recordings or even works of graphic art. Note the concentration on *areas of work assessed*. In fact this kind of specification forces the issue of what we are assessing: here it is not 'work' or 'thought processes' or in some general sense 'development', but tangible outcomes produced by those things – another lengthy but interesting issue which needs discussion elsewhere.

Planning-and-implementation

A group-project must be resourced in terms of staffing (both physical and financial). We concentrate here, however, on process and outcome in order to show ways in which active management is necessary to and can improve the educational experience, and to indicate some useful elements of the group project scheme manager's toolkit.

Planning-and-implementation are two inseparable management requirements, deliberately hyphenated for reasons which will become apparent.

Foreseeable pitfalls are predicted by good managers, or at least by those who do not want to find themselves in self-inflicted crises. Effective and practical planning can avoid situations such as: tutors or students sched-uled to be in two places at once; tutors scheduled to be where no students appear; tutors not scheduled to be where students appear; client meetings arranged without the knowledge of the client, or tutors, or students; the physical deployment of documentation and other facilities not matching the location of bodies – and other recognizable problems.

The walk-through

The 'walk-through' is an essential planning tool. The manager needs to mentally walk-through every step of the project, focusing on such things as which students will be scheduled to be where, and when; who will attend meetings; how they will be informed as to where and when; which rooms and equipment need to be booked, by whom and when; which documents will be completed and how many by when; how much stu-dent time will be sufficient to complete the project; what tutorial time to allocate; what arrangements should be made for assessment – and so on. It is helpful to generate an actual list of questions which, if answered in advance, will save much of the firefighting that the project manager, tutor or administrator might otherwise have to do.

The walk-through is even more effective if done with a colleague when, hopefully, the dialogue exposes the loopholes. In fact, not least for the managerial planning discipline, it is useful to compile a comprehen-sive handbook in which every element of the scheme is detailed. This can be written as if intended for the student, but will also have a clear implicit tutor briefing function. It can be distributed to all those involved, includ-ing clients where appropriate.

The handbook should represent a sort of toolkit, consisting of instruc-tions or statements or details on, for example, project objectives; princi-ples and rules of conduct; schedules; deadlines; assessment methods and feedback.

Assessment documentation

In any approach to assessment and feedback there is an obvious need to balance the discipline engendered by a proforma approach with the advantages of open and expansive comment. In practice it is a good idea to design a series of proforma assessment and other administrative sheets to encourage the cooperation of all concerned. The simpler the documen-tation the more likely staff are to complete it.

Concluding remarks

There are a range of further issues surrounding group-projects that it has not been possible to raise here. For example, questions remain concerning the human resource management of ongoing educational vehicles and devices; of staff development (on a macro level in scheme management, and a micro level in group-work facilitation). There are also cost implications and issues in the management of resources.

One final point, which reflects a new reality for tutors. If the management of the group-project is successful it is in their own interest to obtain academically respectable research results to demonstrate that, and to publish them. When academic managers present themselves for recognition, manifest managerial or even intellectual excellence is interestingly ranked by comparison with conventional research.

Chapter Nine

The Development of a 'Learning in Groups' Course for Academic Staff

Roy Gregory and Lin Thorley

Introduction

The development of personal transferable skills and student-centred learning are two of the major themes of the Enterprise in Higher Education Initiative at the University of Hertfordshire. Group-work plays a major part in both these themes, yet many staff were initially not experienced in managing group-based learning. A four-day residential course in group skills was therefore introduced, and has now evolved into a central part of the university's academic staff development programme.

The course aims to encourage participants to review the learning process in higher education within the context of working with small groups. For staff to use small groups effectively means developing personal, interpersonal and facilitative skills, plus a change in the student/tutor relationship from the more traditional didactic role towards a 'learning manager' role. The course uses experiential learning both as a model and also as the most fitting method of delivery. Many of the insights and skills needed for group-based learning can only be effectively acquired as part of personal development, facilitated through a participative learning environment.

Development of the course

The 'Learning in Groups' course has been developed over three years from an initial 'Group Skills' course run by external consultants for the original Hatfield Polytechnic Enterprise team. The authors attended the first course and have since tutored it themselves a further seven times. Over 100 members of academic staff have participated overall.

The original course was not specially focused on university lecturers but came from the wider field of management training. When we, as academics, took over, changes were made to give more guidance at the beginning of the course and to introduce a clearer theoretical framework. More emphasis is now given to general educational issues in order to focus the experience more explicitly towards staff teaching in higher education.

The course has evolved well beyond the original design and now has a much stronger emphasis on experiential learning and learning matters in general, in addition to the personal/interpersonal skills involved in group-work and the process of managing task-related groups.

The evolution process has included the authors' own development as tutors, under the guidance of the original course tutors using an 'apprenticeship model'. The development phase included running a joint course with Bradford University (Matthew *et al.*, 1992). This careful development phase proved to be important in producing a quality course and also in giving authority to its formal validation by the university, for, as discussed later, this must include not only the content of the course but also the personal competence and accreditation of the tutors.

Course details

The course aims are addressed by giving participants experience of working in groups, first through working on the personal and interpersonal skills involved and later in designing and running a group exercise. Two days are spent on these basic building blocks of communication in groups. The full course group is then divided into two, with each half asked to design and run a group activity using the other half as 'students'. The course tutors at this point act as observers and encourage the participants to try out the skills they have been working on during the first part of the course. Finally, the whole exercise is evaluated with the tutors.

The participants finish the course having themselves been involved in working in groups and having acted as designers and tutors, in addition to discussing more theoretical aspects of learning and group-work. The course is participative and interactive throughout, with time given to practice in giving and receiving feedback and being able to reflect on the particular learning experiences. Overall this produces a most valuable learning experience.

Each course has been evaluated by questionnaire and open discussion both at the end of the residential and a few weeks later. Participants then join a programme of day and half-day workshops back at the university covering follow-up topics suggested by course members.

Delivery method

The delivery method emphasizes a deep approach to the learning of how to teach and how to deliver quality education, with less emphasis on the skills/technique approach of surface learning. The importance of a deep approach has recently been highlighted by Ramsden (1992; also see Chapter 1 in the present volume).

It is interesting to note that staff who have heavy work loads often demand a surface approach to 'learning to teach' in the same way and for the same reasons that our students do. Staff can often become frustrated when not given the 'hints and tips' they feel they need in order to respond to the pressing demands back at the university (Gregory and Thorley, 1993).

The nature of the course also gives opportunity for feelings about participants' own place in education and their concerns about educational quality to surface and be given attention. This is often the prelude to very productive and creative work being carried out over the four days of the residential course. We feel it is important to build in time for discussion of current issues within higher education and to allow for its frustrations and difficulties to be talked about. The course is therefore discursive as well as having a strongly reflective element.

The residential nature of the course is essential for adequate reflection to occur to create an environment where a deep approach to learning about the issues addressed can be encouraged. The residential aspect not only gives time for staff to concentrate on one topic, time sadly lacking for university lecturers in their everyday work, but also to give the opportunity for the informal interaction necessary to work through the issues which arise on the course. The venue needs to be sufficiently far away from the campus so that the theme is continued without the disturbance of returning for 'that vital meeting'.

An awareness session has been added prior to the residential, and is intended to enable staff to choose whether they wish to join in the course. The ideas of experiential learning and surface and deep approaches to learning used on the course are described and demonstrated and a taster of methods offered. In effect, it becomes a 'matching up' session, in which both sides can decide on the appropriateness of the course for an individual's own particular needs.

Response

The response from participants has been generally very good. It has been very useful for staff new to teaching in higher education and has been complementary to the one-year part-time in-service training course held at the university. More experienced staff have found it an opportunity to acquire new skills, to provide the impetus to change and to recharge their batteries.

The course has also been found particularly useful for staff and curriculum development where a number of colleagues from one particular area of the university have been on the course. For example, seven out of 15 members of academic staff have attended from the division of civil engineering. The head of that division writes:

all have greatly valued the course and group activity is becoming commonly used in the teaching process within the division. Also the teaching and learning process in established group activities such as field courses and design projects has improved because of improved skills in running such activities. The emphasis throughout the course on reflection and feedback has been commented upon as being a valuable learning experience for those taking part.

Group activities can be used to shift the responsibility for learning towards the student. This is not only good for the students, but is also potentially valuable in enabling staff to use their time more effectively.

These comments reflect the way the course has been a significant agent for change. It has generated enthusiasm and motivation among many of the staff that have attended to try new student-centred methods of delivery.

The course has also been helpful in the development of an interdisciplinary design project in the school of engineering. (Hamilton and Gregory, 1991) A one-week project for all second year undergraduates (380 in 1992) has been developed. The key supervisors have been through the 'Learning in Groups' course and bring this experience to the design project.

'Learning in Groups' has given staff time to reflect on such issues as process versus content, assessment of group-work/skills, the importance of feedback and reflection and also given a general appreciation of the operation of task-oriented groups. Many staff have gone away from the course vividly reminded and sensitized to what can happen to individuals, for example in terms of feelings, even in task-oriented groups. They have had emphasized through their own experience the importance of this understanding and sensitivity when working with student groups.

The reaction of participants, as seen in evaluation forms, has generally been very positive and many have subsequently encouraged others to enrol on the course. Many of the most useful stated outcomes on the eval-

The reaction of participants, as seen in evaluation forms, has generally been very positive and many have subsequently encouraged others to enrol on the course. Many of the most useful stated outcomes on the evaluation forms have been in addition to those identified in the course aims. A consistent feature of the questionnaire responses has been scores for 'personal usefulness' which are even higher than the very encouraging scores for specified course aims. The course benefits are generally individual and somewhat unpredictable; this appears to be typical of experiential learning of this type.

Validation

'Learning in Groups' has now been validated as a one-module CATS course for postgraduate programmes leading to PgD, MA and MSc awards. The course has been validated by using one of the original management tutors as one of the evaluators so that the current tutors' competence is included in the validation. Other evaluators were used to obtain input from the fields of education and personal and group counselling.

Validation of courses which rest on experiential learning and thus on process skills must include validation of the competence of the tutors and cannot rely solely on the written content. This involves universities adapting their traditional role in validation if quality of provision is to be maintained.

Concluding remarks

We believe we have developed a course that can make a significant contribution by linking together staff and educational development. The course has given staff a new and powerful experience of group learning, a chance to reflect on their own skills in becoming managers of the learning process and time to discuss at length with colleagues in other discipline areas educational issues of common interest. These benefits require time for a group to be together. Hence the residential nature of the course is essential and could not be replaced adequately by activities on campus.

Such courses are crucial if high quality group-work is to be managed by staff competent in both the process and task aspects of the group-work. Staff skills can only be developed in these areas in the context of their own personal development: this requires the use of experiential learning.

References

Gregory, R and Thorley, L (1993) 'Deep and surface approaches to learning to teach engineering', in *Achieving and Assessing Quality of Engineering Education*, SEFI 20th International Conference Proceedings, Sweden.

Hamilton, P H and Gregory, R D (1991) 'Interdisciplinary design project in innovative teaching in engineering', in Smith, R A (ed.) *Innovative Teaching and Engineering*, Chichester: Ellis Horwood.

Matthew, R G S, Hughes, D G, Gregory, R D and Thorley, L (1992) 'What about the Teacher?' in Duggan, T V (ed.) *Computational Mechanics Publications*, Vol 1, 417–23 .

Ramsden, P (1992) *Learning to Teach in Higher Education*, London: Routledge.

Chapter Ten

The Effects of Group Composition upon Students' Perceptions of Their Learning

C Dawson, P Lord and J Baggott

Introduction

At Thames Valley University, as at many others, the current trend is for the learning environment changing from being one in which individual students operate alone to one in which students participate in groups for a significant proportion of their learning experience. The composition of these groups, in terms of the way the individuals operate within them, has so far been little investigated. Yet at first sight it seems there is likely to be a connection between the composition of a team and its success as measured in learning outcomes.

Belbin's work on management teams (1989) gave us the idea of investigating the effects of group-composition on student learning outcomes, using his classification of 'team-roles'. The work this prompted us to undertake is not yet finished, so that we do not have a definitive answer. Nevertheless, we feel that a description of the process could be useful to others working in this area and certainly raises some interesting issues.

Belbin's team roles

Belbin's work is comparatively well-known but warrants a brief re-visit in this context. His work centres on the effects of management team composition upon team performance. He defines the concept of 'team-role' as: '... the ways in which members with characteristic personalities and abilities contribute to a team'. Belbin uses five interlocking principles to guide his work:

- Members of a management team can contribute in two ways to the achievement of team objectives. They can perform well in a functional role in drawing on their professional and technical knowledge as the situation demands. They also have potentially valuable team-roles to perform. A team-role describes a pattern of behaviour characteristic of the way in which one team member interacts with others in facilitating the progress of the team.
- Each team needs an optimum balance in both functional roles and team-roles. The ideal blend will depend on the goals and tasks the team faces.
- Team effectiveness will be promoted by the extent to which members correctly recognize and adjust themselves to the relative strengths within the team both in expertise and ability to engage in specific team-roles.
- Personal qualities fit members for some team-roles while limiting the likelihood that they will succeed in others.
- A team can deploy its technical resources to best advantage only when it has the requisite range of team-roles to ensure efficient team-work.

Through his research Belbin identified eight team-roles, and also devised an instrument, the 'Self-perception inventory' (SPI) which he claims can be used to identify the team-role which best describes the individual completing it.

However, Belbin's work is concerned with the performance of the group, rather than with the learning achieved by the members of the group. From a teaching and learning perspective there may be a relationship between group performance and individual learning, in which case the performance of the group may be seen as an intervening or moderating variable between group composition and individual learning outcome. Equally there may be a more direct relationship between group composition and individual learning. We decided to investigate this, using the hypothesis that students working in 'balanced' groups will report the achievement of superior learning outcomes compared to students working in groups of random selection.

The research design

The student group used in this work is the certificate in management (CM) group. This is a one-year programme, with most participants progressing onto a diploma in management studies. The students are mature part-timers, almost all employed, mainly in junior or middle management, with about 60 per cent being graduates.

CM students attend two residential weekends during their course, with about 30 students on each. The first of these weekends is used to collect the data for this study. The theme of this weekend is 'interpersonal and group behaviour'. The weekend is divided into eight learning sessions running from Friday evening through to Sunday lunchtime. The exercises in all sessions involve students operating as members of groups. At the start of the weekend students are given Belbin's SPI to complete and are told that this is to help them think about their own characteristics and behaviour as members of working groups. It is also made clear that they will get feedback on the inventory at a later stage. Completed forms are collected and analysed by staff.

Students are also asked to complete 'Exercise Evaluation Sheets' for each session, it being explained that these have two main purposes. They provide individuals with a structured way of reviewing and reflecting on the exercise and also provide information for staff on the effectiveness of the exercises. No specific reference is made to the hypothesis we are working on.

The first exercise acts as a trial run, with students allocated to groups on a random basis. Of the remaining exercises during the weekend, four are used as key exercises. These are exercises from which clear group performance measures are obtainable. For each of these an 'experimental group' is put together, using the information from the SPI so that the group will include all the team-roles identified by Belbin among its members. The remaining students are allocated to control groups on a random basis. This process is repeated for the other three key exercises, wherever possible different individuals being used within the experimental group. Apart from in very exceptional circumstances (for example, only one student among the 30 at that weekend belonging to a particular Belbin team-role type) no student will be a member of the experimental group for all key exercises.

The key exercises

The first of these is the 'Committee exercise'. This is concerned with group decision making with respect to resource allocation. The group task is to allocate a small amount of money as salary awards to six staff members, with thumbnail biographical sketches provided. Roles are allocated, as either chairperson or the superior of the staff whose salary increases are to be determined. Forty-five minutes are allowed for the exercise, and groups are told they are in competition. At the end of the session group performance is evaluated, with all subjects scoring the performance of other groups. By aggregation a final score for each group can be determined.

The second, 'Barrels exercise', involves group problem solving. Teams of four to six begin by planning a route of planks spanning oil barrels across an aircraft hangar strewn with obstacles. Each obstacle crossed gives the team a task to complete, the tasks being of varying difficulty according to a colour-code. Once the planning session is over teams submit their plans and are issued with the tasks. These involve sorting and classifying various types of information. The total time taken for a team to complete all its tasks is recorded and added to the number of planks laid, yielding an overall score for each team. The winning team is the one with the lowest score.

The third exercise is the familiar 'NASA survival exercise', involving individual and group decision making. All participants rank a series of items for usefulness in the event of their spaceship crash-landing on the moon. Participants then form into groups, which are to arrive at a consensus ranking of the same items. Each participant then calculates the difference between their score, the group consensus score and an 'expert' score, prepared by NASA scientists.

The final key exercise is the again well-known 'Prisoner's dilemma'. This involves inter- and intra-group decision making. Overall group performance is measured by the closing bank balance of each group.

Exercise proformas

Two proformas are used to collect data for this study. The first is the 'Exercise evaluation sheet'. This asks eight questions about students' perceived learning experiences in the exercise. Responses are scored on a seven-point Likert-type scale, indicating agreement or disagreement for each statement. An additional open-ended question is also provided at the end of the questionnaire. The respondent's individual identity is not known, but the group they belong to is recorded, making it possible to distinguish between responses from members of experimental groups and control groups.

The second proforma is the 'Exercise ranking sheet', which all participants complete at the end of the weekend. This sheet entails ranking all exercises taken part in during the weekend. Ranking is according to the individuals' perception of the relevance and interest of the exercises. Respondents are asked to identify themselves.

From the data derived from the 'Exercise evaluation sheet' it is possible to discern on which dimensions, if any, subjects from experimental groups and control groups rate each exercise differently. Similarly, from the data derived from the 'Exercise ranking sheet' it is possible to discern whether participation in an experimental group leads to a higher ranking of an exercise than does participation in a control group.

Review and discussion of the research

At the time of writing this research is still at the stage of data collection, so it is not yet possible to review any findings. There are, however, some interesting points which may act as a basis for discussion.

The first relates to the subjects of the research and the environment in which the data are collected. These are all mature management students studying on a part-time basis. The question is the extent to which any findings may be generalized to other types of learners and other types of learning environment.

The second point relates to the design of the study and its relationship to Belbin's work. Within the study, group membership (for both control and experimental groups) is varied for each session. With each session lasting approximately one and a half hours (of which only part of the time would involve direct participation in the group exercise) there is a limited amount of time for individuals to establish their team-role identities. Questions arise as to whether there is a minimum time period required for team-roles to be established in any group, and whether in the exercises from which data are collected such a threshold time is reached.

The third point is to acknowledge that what is being investigated in this research is individuals' perceptions of the learning derived from participation in certain exercises rather than learning *per se*; and moreover, that these are the perceptions obtained immediately after the exercises have been completed. Perceptions may alter with the passage of time and as a result of individuals' subsequent experiences, both of which may be significant factors influencing the subjects' learning. Questions raised here include those relating to the reliability and validity of the data generated particularly from the 'Exercise evaluation sheets' and the relationship if any between such self-reports and the occurrence of learning.

Notwithstanding these points, in deciding whether group composition makes a difference to subjects' perceptions of their learning it is necessary to show that statistically significant differences are reported by members of control and experimental groups. If this is found to be the case it is then necessary to determine whether overall group performance is a significant variable in students' reported perceived learning. If this too is the case, then the nature of this variable must also be investigated. Group performance may be an intervening or moderating variable, or may indeed be an independent variable. We believe that with the design adopted we will obtain the necessary data to adequately investigate these relationships.

Reference

Belbin, R M (1989) *Management Teams: Why they succeed or fail*, Oxford: Heinemann.

Chapter Eleven

Peer Evaluation in Practice: Experience from a Major Group Project

Brian Mathews

Introduction

This chapter describes the development and use of peer evaluation in a diploma in management studies (DMS) group project at the University of Teesside. The peer evaluation involves group members in assessing the contribution of both themselves and each other on a variety of dimensions. There is no requirement for agreement of the final results: each person's assessment is made independently and in confidence. Peer evaluation feeds into the overall examination process, one of its main uses being as a mechanism to ensure equitable distribution of grades within a group.

The move into peer evaluation was stimulated by a revision of the DMS programme. Formerly, personal interviews had been held to establish (amongst other things) individual contributions. This was recognized as ineffective and a more reliable, formal system was sought.

Context and background of the group-project

Over the last 20 years the DMS group-project has evolved into a sophisticated and substantial part of the Teesside programme and is now its major distinctive feature. It is seen as a highly valuable element of the programme.

The project has four key characteristics: it is group-based; it is conducted for an external organization (but not for the employer of any group member); it addresses a real management problem; and it is a substantial piece of work. The project's group nature encourages individual personal development.

The whole ethos of the second year of the DMS programme is in fact based on group-work and group development. It takes a group of usually four individuals 15 weeks of part-time study with no other classes running. The main project thus accounts for about one quarter of the total DMS – hence the need for reliability in assessment.

Project assessment and the role of peer evaluation

Assessment of the group-project falls into two main areas: first, appraisal of a consultant-style report submitted on completion of the project, plus a video presentation of five to seven minutes duration; and second, self- and peer assessment of learning from, and contribution to, the project activity.

Responsibility for the final assessment rests with two markers; in this case they are members of staff, one normally the project tutor. They establish both the baseline of assessment (a grade for the work) and determine any variation in grade between individuals in the group. The latter issue is more emotive than the former. It relies on the tutors' (examiners') knowledge of the individuals in the group, on factual evidence provided by the group or individual members, and on peer assessment. The peer and self-assessments provide valuable input for the assessment process (Brown and Dove, 1991) but are not the sole means of differentiation between individuals.

Development of the evaluation form

Having moved away from personal interviews for evaluating the relative inputs of individual students there was a need to develop a robust means of measurement. Drawing on existing work (Rackham *et al.*, 1971) and in collaboration with colleagues and students a suitable tool was evolved.

The document examines group processes under two headings: *task management* (behaviours that move the group towards completion of its working goals) and *process management* (behaviours that determine the quality of the relationships between the group members). Each of these topics is further divided into several sub-sections. While group processes represent a very important aspect of the activity it is not a complete picture. Also included are considerations of the *project output* (contribution to the task in terms of time and/or effort and/or quality) and an *overall evaluation* category.

In designing the form the use of different types of scale was considered. The constant sum technique was adopted, as it offers considerable advantages in that it communicates the relative importance of a number of attributes. This is particularly appropriate where differential judgements need to be made (Appel and Jackson, 1975). A copy of the form is shown in Figure 11.1 at the end of this chapter. In addition to the form itself students are given full instructions for completing it, including definition of the terms and roles used.

Issues raised

The implementation of any new technique is a time for learning and review. A range of issues became apparent from the results of the first peer evaluation.

There were two styles of response in coming to an overall evaluation: some students gave an 'out of ten' rating, others added up the ratings of all 15 items. The former was intended, but the difficulties caused by the latter were not great. Of more concern was the existence of five different patterns of response.

- *Equality:* group members are so sure that they all contributed equally that they all give ratings of 10 points for each and every area. Group members seem concerned here not to provide any information that might be detrimental to their fellows.
- *Normal distribution:* group members attribute a rating of between five and 15 on the dimensions. Although it seems unlikely that there is a genuine equality of input, group pressure and people's goodwill make this the most common alternative. It demonstrates give and take within a group and a sensible distribution of workload and responsibility.
- *The reluctant finger:* where there has been free-wheeling on the part of one member the responses from other members show a consistent level of under-contribution for that person. This may be mirrored by the individual's self-rating. It seems that in most cases people will bend over backwards not to 'shop' their friends. Where there is a real reduction in ratings, therefore, this should be taken seriously by the examiners.
- *Stitch them up:* sometimes, however, there can seem to be collusion between some of the group members. This is characterized by an over-similar pattern of evaluations giving a clear indication of poor performance on the part of one individual. This pattern is perhaps the most

difficult to deal with as a tutor. If there is a systematic victimization of one individual then perhaps there is a good argument to penalize the group as a whole.

● *Out of kilter:* perceptions vary between individuals. From time to time there can be cases where the pattern of response varies considerably within the group. The simplest case is where someone thinks that they have done considerably more than anyone else. If this is so then averaging the reports of others can give a more consistent evaluation.

The hardest decision to arrive at is to fail one individual and pass the rest of the group. The ratings show a quantitative evaluation of group members' feelings concerning each other. Adverse ratings, either on an overall basis or on individual items, need to be taken fully into account. The numbers require interpretation within the context of the project and the group.

The project is after all a group project. If individuals do not contribute to the group then this undermines its entire ethos. The DMS emphasizes the role of the group and many elements of the taught part prepare the individual for this stage. In the final event, examiners must be satisfied that variations in grades are a fair reflection of the information available to them at the time.

Conclusions and further development

The experience of using peer assessment has uncovered a variety of issues. There is a clear need for continuing development from both the perspective of the institution (in terms of assessment) and of the participants (in terms of preparedness).

Following its first use the form itself was found to be satisfactory apart from one small adjustment. The instructions also needed tightening. However, there are still problems with interpretation of the scale which may not be easy to resolve totally. Also, the form itself had only been finalized shortly before the end of the project and an important lesson was learned here about the need to have assessment tools in place from the beginning.

Individuals wishing to claim a substantial variation in grade must provide the evidence on which to base a case. It is clear, however, that the peer evaluation form is not enough on its own to cause a fail grade to be awarded.

An external examiners' board may not be sufficiently in tune with the process of peer evaluation to be entirely satisfied with the result. This is especially true if the final decision is to fail one student or if the set of forms is incomplete. The system is robust and can support a fail decision provided all students have had the opportunity to participate. As a final point, peer assessment is a part of the process, not the total.

References

Appel, V and Jackson, B (1975) 'Copy testing in a comparative environment', *Journal of Marketing*, 21, August, 84–6.

Brown, S and Dove, P (1991) *Self and Peer Assessment*, Standing Conference on Educational Development, Paper 63, Birmingham: SCED.

Rackham, N, Honey, P and Colbert, M (1971) *Developing Interactive Skills*, Northampton: Wellens Publishing.

DMS PROJECT PEER GROUP EVALUATION FORM

Your Name	_____
Member 2	_____
Member 3	_____
Member 4	_____
Member 5	_____
Member 6	_____

Peer Group Ratings –
Please rate the contribution of each group member on the dimensions below. The total on each row must equal the number of team members times ten; i.e. for four members the total score for all members must be 40.

Project Output	You	2	3	4	5	6
Ideas for the Project						
Background Reading						
Collecting Data						
Analysis and Interpretation						
Writing the Report						
Task Management						
Initiating						
Seeking Information and Opinions						
Giving Information or Opinions						
Clarifying and Elaborating						
Summarising						
Consensus Testing						
Process Management						
Confronting Self and Others						
Gate Keeping						
Encouraging						
Standard Setting and Testing						
Overall Evaluation						

Figure 11.1 *Student peer group evaluation form*

Using group-work to encourage student autonomy

In order to maximize students' motivation and to encourage their ability to continue to learn after they leave higher education it is important to work towards student autonomy. Group-work offers one way of encouraging autonomy and the chapters in this section give examples of how this can be promoted.

Katherine Cuthbert from the Manchester Metropolitan University reflects on part of a course in communication and group behaviour which contributes to a BA in Applied Social Studies by Independent Study. The course gives students experience in being in a group and then encourages them to make links between this and theoretical behaviour studies in other course units. The students report favourably on the experience. Positive student response is, incidentally, most common where the group process is, as here, itself part of the course content.

Peter Cuthbert from the same university describes self-development groups used as part of a DMS programme. The groups tackle case studies in one term and operate as learning sets for action learning in the following term. In their second year groups tackle a consultancy exercise for a client organization. A variety of tasks focus on the group, individual and task needs and provide an environment for autonomous self-development.

Courses in chemical engineering at the University of Teesside described by Bainbridge use problem-based learning in groups, asking students to construct their own curriculum as the need arises in response to a series of graded problems. These courses involve tutors in changing the way they work, particularly in that they necessitate their working in teams and with flexible timetables.

The use of learning journals on a health visiting and nursing programme at the University of East London is reported by Marjorie Talbot. A short description of the history of nurse education at the beginning of this chapter allows one to make an interesting link between the long-established culture of a discipline and student response to new methods. The course described involves both a traditionally taught element and student group-led seminars. Students are given training in working in groups and use journals designed to assist their learning process.

McNally at the University of Glasgow gives an overview of the use of group-work, centring on a graduate recruitment perspective. He describes some of the work done under the Enterprise Initiative, with examples from law, history, mathematics and student training of class representatives. Group-work is seen as promoting many of the transferable skills that employers say they want graduates to have, and that graduates themselves will find will aid their autonomy in future life-roles.

Chapter Twelve

Facilitating Understanding of Group Dynamics

Katherine Cuthbert

Background

In higher education group-based learning has traditionally entailed group discussion in the tutorial or seminar context. More recently group-based project work is becoming much more common. One of the important objectives of such project work is to provide students with the experience of working as group members and hopefully developing associated skills.

However there is perhaps another, complementary, way of acquiring the skills of working as a member of a group. This would derive from learning about the structure and functioning of groups. There is a considerable body of knowledge, arising primarily from social psychology, which is concerned with understanding how groups function. But to learn about groups is almost certainly not sufficient to support the aim of skilled understanding. Such knowledge could be acquired in a somewhat abstract and impersonal way with a primarily surface understanding (Gibbs, 1992). A more appropriate aim would be to provide a context in which students can use such knowledge to develop the kind of understanding which has personal relevance and provides a framework within which they can reflect upon their own feelings, reactions and responses in relation to their own interpersonal and group-based behaviour.

This chapter discusses an attempt to provide such a personally relevant context in which students can learn about group processes and dynamics. The unit involved is called 'Communication and group behaviour', and it contributes to the BA in Applied Social Studies by Independent Study at the Crewe and Alsager faculty of the Manchester Metropolitan University. It complements other units in the degree within which students are engaged in group-based project work.

Syllabus, aims and rationale

Before examining the group-based learning which is part of 'Communication and group behaviour' it is important to provide some comment on the general nature of the unit. It has the overall aim of using content from humanistic and social psychology to promote awareness of reactions and responses within the group and interpersonal context.

The unit content is divided into three main sections: group structure and dynamics; self-understanding and self-management; and interpersonal interaction and communication. It is the first of these which is of particular interest in this context. Specific topics include the nature of groups, norms, group cohesiveness, 'group think', deviance, group goals, cooperation and competition, management of conflict, and leadership. These topics have been selected with the intention of having a relevance to how groups actually work, rather than being of just academic interest.

Thus the main concern is to provide a learning context within which students can make direct links between the academic content and the actual experience of working and functioning as a member of an active group, and to encourage personal reflection upon these experiences. (See Boud *et al.*, 1985, for further justification of the encouragement of reflection in relation to experiential learning and Cuthbert, 1992, for an account of the use of his model as a basis for this unit.)

Three main features of the teaching/learning framework have been adopted to attempt to achieve these aims. First, and centrally, students are actively involved each week in an experiential exercise which aims to illustrate some particular aspect of group dynamics. Second, the relevant literature is discussed in student-led groups – the expectation is that such discussion will provide a better opportunity for students to link academic content to their own experience than could be possible within any kind of lecture set-up. The third feature concerns the provision of assessment which is appropriate to the aims of the unit in that it encourages reflection on personal functioning within the group situation.

Experiential Group-work

Experiential group-work provides the central core for the teaching of the unit. It provides practical illustration of the academic content which supports the unit and requires the active involvement of students.

Experiential exercises of this kind are quite frequently used in various areas of professional education and training and to some extent within the more structured, group-based approaches to personal growth. There are a number of published sources which provide descriptions of such exercises. Prominent among these are the handbooks of Pfeiffer and Jones, beginning in 1974, which essentially consist of a collection of such exercises, and the volume by Johnson and Johnson (1990), which provides a more limited set of exercises but with more extended comment on the nature of group processes.

My task in selecting exercises for use in the academic context has been to identify those which have a clear relevance to the available literature on group processes. The exercises used are of various kinds but usually involve some kind of role-play, simulation or problem-solving activity. They are intended to be enjoyable and absorbing in themselves but also provide a basis for further thought.

In order to promote such reflection the debriefing discussion at the end of the exercise is of considerable importance (see also Pearson and Smith, 1985). Students are encouraged to share their reactions to and feelings about the exercise experience. Discussion is promoted through the use of two supporting procedures. First, for many exercises students complete a brief post-exercise questionnaire which encourages them to focus on important aspects of the interaction within the exercise. Second, most exercises use observers as well as participants. In the debriefing discussion after the exercise observers can often provide a somewhat different perspective on the exercise process.

It may be helpful to provide a brief overview of one of the exercises which is used within the unit. 'Stranded in the desert', adapted from Johnson and Johnson, has the aim of providing an exercise situation within which students can explore the role of conflict in problem solving and decision making. It is assumed that controversy, disagreement and argument have both costs and benefits and the exercise is designed to promote consideration of how these can be both effectively managed, but also easily mismanaged. This exploration develops out of earlier considerations of conformity, cohesion, 'group think' and deviance.

The exercise sets up a scenario in which some participants are encouraged to argue for one solution to their survival dilemma, while others argue for another. If nobody gives way deadlock is likely to ensue. On the other hand, if there is a flexible examination of different positions and a willingness to combine ideas in new ways, it is more likely that an appropriate consensus decision will be reached. Groups vary in the way in which they respond to this decision-making situation but, whatever the nature of this response, it can be a useful basis for discussion of how controversy can be most constructively managed.

Student-led Discussion Groups

At the beginning of each weekly session students spend time discussing the reading they have done over the previous week. This reading links with and draws upon the exercise which was completed within the last class session. These discussions are conducted in small student-led groups (around five students). Such groups allow, indeed require, greater student participation, and provide students with an opportunity to actively work through and exchange ideas. They provide, in a sense, a form of peer-tutoring in which students are able to help each other towards a better understanding (Jaques, 1992). This is particularly important in an area where students are encouraged to reflect on experience, as well as develop their understanding of the relevant literature.

Another important reason for making use of student-led discussion groups within this unit is that they provide participants with a further opportunity to experience group interaction and dynamics, this time in a real rather than simulated context.

Students are expected, on a rotating basis, to take up the roles of chairperson and rapporteur to a plenary session. As the unit progresses they will be asked to consider how they are managing their own group within this discussion context.

Assessment

As has been indicated the purpose of the unit is to promote reflective personal understanding of interpersonal and group dynamics. It is important that the assessment procedures used within the unit support this aim. From this point of view one of the most crucial parts of the overall assessment involves the keeping of a weekly journal which encourages the student to reflect in writing on their own experience and reactions within the unit (see also Rainer, 1980 and Walker, 1985). However it is probably most appropriate that such a document is primarily a private one. It is therefore assessed on a pass-fail basis only, and provided that it fulfils certain basic requirements (for example, making comment on a given minimum of exercises) then it will obtain a pass grading.

However, students are encouraged to use their journal record as a basis for the preparation of an 'Evaluative review of personal learning'. In this review they are expected to discuss analytically and reflectively what they have learned about themselves and their own behaviour, feelings and interactional responses from the experience of the unit.

The expectation is that the review will be written at the end of the unit and will require students to examine retrospectively their personal experience within the unit and in relation to relevant literature (see Cuthbert, 1993, for a more detailed examination of assessment procedures used within the unit.)

Evaluation and future potential

Student reaction to this unit has been and continues to be positive. At a superficial level this results from many of the experiential exercises being enjoyable and often entertaining and providing an interesting change from more usual teaching approaches. At a more fundamental level students comment that the unit has helped to develop their personal confidence, provided them with a better understanding of their interpersonal behaviour, led to changed responses in the group context and that they have been able to apply learning derived from within the unit to other relevant situations.

However, given the current pressure in relation to resources, student numbers and tutor time in higher education, it is important to review the success and value of this approach to teaching in rather different ways. In the past the unit has run with relatively small numbers (up to about 15); this year it is running with a group of 23. Some practical problems are being experienced: most particularly, the plenary session which follows the student-led discussion groups is probably less successful with the larger groups.

The intention is to experiment with other strategies for concluding such discussion (for example, using posters to display summary results of discussion, or representatives of one group moving on to another to report on their discussion; see Jaques, 1992). My present judgement is that given appropriate accommodation, it would be possible to make use of these teaching strategies with rather larger groups of students.

Another recent development relates to the induction of new tutors into the teaching of the unit. The approaches now used on the unit have developed through some degree of trial and error over a period of time. But they are now quite well structured, and as a result it has been possible to explain the nature and aims of the unit to other tutors with relatively little difficulty. Undoubtedly, the discipline of writing about the unit, as here, itself plays a part in the developmental and clarification process.

References

Boud, D, Keogh, R and Walker, D (1985) 'Promoting reflection in learning: a model', in Boud, D, Keogh, R and Walker, D (eds) *Using Experience into Learning*, London: Kogan Page.

Cuthbert, K (1992) 'Can we teach social skills within the undergraduate psychology curriculum? An approach using experiential exercises and promoting reflective awareness', *Psychology Teaching Review*, 1, 2, 57–65.

Cuthbert, K (1993) 'Records of achievement in relation to personal learning', in Assiter, A and Shaw, E (eds) *Using Records of Achievement in Higher Education*, London: Kogan Page.

Gibbs, G (1992) *Improving the Quality of Student Learning*, Bristol: Technical and Educational Services Limited.

Jaques, D (1992) *Learning in Groups*, 2nd edn, London: Kogan Page.

Johnson, D W and Johnson, F P (1990) *Joining Together: Group theory and group skills*, 4th edn, New Jersey: Prentice-Hall.

Pearson, M and Smith, D (1985) 'Debriefing in experience-based learning' in Boud, D, Keogh, R and Walker, D (eds) *Reflection: Turning experience into learning*, London: Kogan Page.

Pfeiffer, J W and Jones, J E (1974) *A Handbook of Structured Experiences for Human Relationship Training*, Vol I, La Jolla, CA: University Associates.

Rainer, T (1980) *The New Diary: How to use a journal*, London: Angus and Robertson/Harper Collins.

Walker, D (1985) 'Writing and reflection', in Boud, D, Keogh, R and Walker, D (eds) *Reflection: Turning experience into learning*, London: Kogan Page.

Chapter Thirteen

Self-development Groups on a Diploma in Management Studies Course

Peter Cuthbert

Introduction

The Department of Business and Management Studies at the Crewe and Alsager Faculty of the Manchester Metropolitan University has now enrolled the fourth cohort of its self-development based Diploma in Management Studies (DMS). Two key concepts underlie the course. The first is that the process and practice of management is very much about the working of groups or teams. The second is that managers need to gain the skill of self-development if they are to progress in their careers.

Group-working is central to the DMS. In the first year groups operate as self-development groups, while in the second year the groups form action learning sets. The latter are different in their approach in that they are essentially about task-focused team work in which the final product is as important as the learning which goes on. In self-development groups the focus is more on identifying the individual's learning needs and meeting them through the activities of the group.

Self-development groups

The idea of management self-development groups is not new. They first developed in the USA (Pedler, 1986, p. 6) and have since been adopted for education purposes in the UK and elsewhere. In the management education setting,

the self-development approach is concerned with meeting the learning needs not only ... which arise from the immediate job, but those which will enable ... [the learner] ... to respond to a range of eventualities which may arise during the course of their career (Fisher, 1987, p. 38).

Thus the group can be seen as an enabling mechanism rather than simply as a team acquiring a body of knowledge.

An essential element is that the group and the students take 'ownership' of the learning process rather than being 'taught' in the traditional manner. That is not to say that lectures do not occur but rather that the students play an active role in negotiating the agenda and how it should be delivered.

The role of the staff on ... (such a programme is) ... one of helping individuals learn more effectively from their day to day situations by acting as a 'catalyst' through which learning opportunities can be exploited (Fisher, op cit., p. 39).

The aim is to equip the student with a body of learning skills that will be useful long after the 'knowledge' content of the course has become obsolete. This approach is very much in accord with the views of Higher Education for Capability where the discipline forms a vehicle in which to develop learning skills.

The development of such learning skills does not necessarily occur spontaneously. There is a need to create an appropriate forum in which these skills are learned and practised. Old approaches to learning need to be confronted and new patterns of behaviour adopted. Fisher cites five main steps:

- establishment of a supportive learning climate – this is attempted through the use of the self-development groups, innovative approaches to course delivery and the use of personal tutors and in-company mentors;
- assessment of learning needs and setting of goals – training in this difficult task is provided by means of initial class instruction plus a residential weekend early in the course;
- planning, actions and implementation – planning is encouraged on the first residential weekend and the first assessed task involves the preparation of a personal learning plan. In addition, the groups have to prepare group learning plans. All the students have an in-company mentor

who can help set up appropriate learning experiences in the workplace;

- monitor progress – in this case the personal tutor has a role to play as well as the student's mentor and the module tutors;
- evaluate and reassess goals – students keep a personal development file in which they reflect upon their goals and progress. They are also encouraged to redefine learning contracts with the help of their mentor and personal tutor.

The use of groups within the course

Both years of the course consist of six blocks of approximately equal length. This structure was adopted to facilitate delivery since the course is offered on a part-time basis with attendance either on one afternoon and one evening or on two evenings per week.

Self-development is introduced in the early lectures of the course and is the focus for the first residential weekend which occurs after approximately three weeks. In the run up to this weekend students complete a number of standard assessment instruments designed to assess their learning style and their perception of learning opportunities (Honey, 1989; Honey and Mumford, 1989).

The self-development groups can have an important role to play in determining the course materials in the blocks and the method of delivery. Ideally the content studied in each topic area is related to the learning needs of the groups. Similarly the approach to learning should be negotiated and arranged to suit the groups' preferences. This means that the first meeting between a block tutor and the groups will consist of a discussion where the available syllabus is discussed and an appropriate 'menu' chosen, unless this has been done by prior negotiation. Individual students are able to submit to the examination board a portfolio to claim exemption from areas of the course in which they have prior knowledge at an appropriate level.

Assessment is a mixture of peer, mentor and tutor assessment based on course work and examinations. Groups also have a role in producing work for assessment in two areas. The first is in the human resource management module where a group project is required. The second area is where each of the groups develops a problem solving case study based around real problems in the students' own organizations. The case studies are usually based on one student's organization, but some interesting fictional case studies have been prepared which draw upon a number of the organizations represented in a group.

The case studies are used to relate the indicative course content, as for example using critical path analysis, to students' organizations during the problem solving and decision making weekend residential which occurs in the summer term. During this weekend the groups work on about five case studies. Each of the groups present their own case study to the rest of the cohort and set them the task of solving it. Not only does the presenting group have to manage the running of the exercise, the provision of supporting materials and feedback, but also they must assess the quality of the solutions offered by the other groups.

The self-development groups change their role in the second year of the course when they become action learning sets. In this case the focus moves from the development of the individual's perceived learning needs to the development of the whole group's skills with a specific business problem. To achieve this the groups carry out a consultancy exercise of a strategic nature for a client organization.

Choosing the members for the groups

Pedler (1986, p.12) suggests that there are five stages through which self-development groups must go: making contact, exploration, getting down to it, work, finishing. He points out that the groups can disband or fall apart between any of these stages. The end of each stage represents a crisis point at which the group is poised to go either up or down.

If the self-development group is to work successfully it is essential to try to prevent the groups falling apart when the going gets tough. The students are not encouraged to select their own group as they are generally all strangers when they enrol at the start of the first year. Instead the groups are selected by the course tutor on the basis of each student's background and their responses to the 'Group roles preference inventory' (Belbin, 1981). In his study of success and failure of management groups he reported that the most successful groups were those which had a balanced mix of team roles. Experience using this instrument with other courses has shown that this is true for students as well.

Experience of the self-development approach

There is a growing body of literature concerned with self-development and autonomous learning (for example, Boud, 1988; Entwistle and Ramsden, 1983; Gibbs, 1992; Meyer and Parsons, 1989). The following paragraphs distil some of the ideas from the literature so as to provide a benchmark against which our experience at Crewe may be compared.

The Tutors' Role

There seems to be general agreement that tutors have several roles to play:

- manager creating a supporting and stimulating learning environment;
- provision of limits (institutional and standards for the discipline);
- group resource/trainer providing information/skills;
- group member participating and developing with the group;

- group adviser on personal and group issues.

The advantages and disadvantages of using self-development groups for tutors include:

Advantages

- more stimulating than lectures due to varied student needs;
- more personal interaction with small groups;
- self-growth as part of a group;
- might reduce class contact hours.

Disadvantages

- needs a greater breadth of knowledge to help groups;
- greater risk as power is devolved and 'all-knowing expert' role abandoned;
- requires adoption of new (for many) approaches to teaching;
- requires considerable organization to set up and monitor.

The Students' Role

The students' role with self-development groups is rather different to the 'traditional' student role. They too have several hats to wear and can no longer be passive recipients of the lecturer's wisdom. Student roles include:

- active learner;
- reflective evaluator of their own strengths and weaknesses;
- positive group member supporting the group;
- good communicator participating in the group;
- good time manager so the group is on time.

The advantages and disadvantages for students include:

Advantages

- being able to talk to someone when you have a problem;
- hearing different perspectives and ideas aids understanding;
- not feeling alone and isolated;
- sharing of notes, books and information;
- moral support, confidence building and a feeling of belonging;
- makes studying more interesting.

Disadvantages

- the need to learn to work in a group;
- finding time to meet yet still see family;
- transport and communication problems;
- freeriders and unbalanced contributions to group;
- potential clashes of personality;
- dealing with incoming/outgoing group members;
- need to adopt a new learning style.

The Learning Process

The work of Entwistle and Ramsden (1983), Boud (1988), Meyer and Parsons (1989) and others makes it clear that the effective self-developer must necessarily adopt a 'meaning orientation' as their learning style. As Higgs (1988) points out, this is not necessarily the 'natural' style which management students will adopt. Not only will many of the students have to learn how to adopt this approach, they will also have to see that they can safely abandon their former 'reproducing approach'.

In order for this to happen the students need to have the following perceptions of the course:

- the self-development group is as much about developing personal skills as about answering task-based assignments in groups;
- the workload is not so heavy that experiments in self-development cannot be tried and evaluated;
- the assessments on the course reward higher the self-developer using the meaning approach than those who adopt a reproducing approach;
- the tutorial staff understand, support and practise the philosophy of self-development in their course delivery;
- the self-development approach is relevant and beneficial to students in the workplace.

Participants' views

The views of current second-year students, past students and staff were canvassed to establish to what extent the actual course experience matches the predictions of the literature. The results of the canvas are given below.

The Tutor's Role

There seemed to be general agreement between the sample of students and the staff over the tutors' role at Crewe:

- manager role – none of the students believed that their self-develoment tutor played a management role, nor did the staff see themselves as having this role;
- standard-setting – there was agreement that it is the tutors who are responsible for setting standards for the discipline;
- group 'technical' resource – all the staff saw themselves as having a role as a technical resource which could be used by groups. The students, however, disagreed on this. Just over half (54 per cent) saw tutors as a resource while most of the rest (42 per cent) did not; a few were unsure;
- participating group member – most of the students (67 per cent) and all of the tutors felt that staff were not participating members of the groups. However, a significant group of students (25 per cent) believed that staff played this role;
- group adviser – most of the students (70 per cent) felt this was a role played by tutors and so did all the tutors. The remainder of the sample disagreed.

The Students' Role

Identifying students' views of themselves as learners was more difficult than identifying the tutors' roles. In an attempt to get more honest answers some indirect questions were asked:

- active learner – the students were very positive over the issue of preferring active self-development to passive lectures (50 per cent to 38 per cent);
- reflective learner – interestingly nearly all the students (88 per cent) felt that the self-development group was a useful vehicle for meeting their own learning needs. The process of identifying needs was not seen as a difficulty for just over half the students (54 per cent);
- positive group member – from the comments made it would appear that some of the cohort do not take group membership seriously. It was not possible to quantify the extent to which this occurs;
- good communicator – this was not raised as an issue, although some students commented that a strong personality could dominate a group and silence other members;
- time management – the problem raised was the time spent getting together rather than the management of time.

Advantages – the advantages suggested by the students included all those proposed in the literature. Mutual support, shared problem solving and hearing alternative views were mentioned most often.

Disadvantages – all the disadvantages from the literature were suggested by the students with the exception of dealing with new group members and the need to adopt a new learning style. The latter was hinted at by several respondents who suggested that the process can initially be confusing as people 'don't know what they are supposed to be doing or why'. Related to this, one student mentioned the need to be able to make and receive constructive criticism, which is not something that people normally do.

Another respondent suggested that 'waiting for group members to catch up' was a problem. As mentioned above, a related comment was that some group members did not take the process seriously. The most commonly mentioned problem was that of freeriders and inadequate contributions by some members.

Two areas were suggested by the students which are not mentioned in the literature. The first is the problem of dominant personalities and personality clashes in the group. The second is the issue of the isolation of the group members from the rest of the cohort.

The Learning Process

This section produced a few surprises:

- choice of group members – most students (60 per cent) agreed that it was a good idea for the course team to select the self-development group members, while a minority (15 per cent) disagreed. One or two commented that it would have been difficult to self-select a group very early in the course. The risk of the failure of the self-development process due to a combination of personalities and work pressure was also mentioned;
- developing personal skills – the majority of the staff felt that students saw self-development groups as a means of developing personal skills. Of the students questioned, 63 per cent were in accord with the staff view while 33 per cent felt the groups were all about task problem solving;
- workload – staff and student opinions differed on this issue. Half of the students (50 per cent) felt that they did not have the 'space' in which to develop new approaches to learning while 42 per cent felt that they did. Staff generally felt that there was sufficient 'space', but contradicted themselves by suggesting that the student workload was heavy;
- rewards for the meaning approach – students were split on the issue of whether a reproducing approach (54 per cent) or a meaning approach (38 per cent) would achieve the greatest rewards for the assessments. Two-thirds of the staff were of the opinion that a reproducing approach would not be sufficient to guarantee success in their assessment. These symmetrical but conflicting views suggest that the staff need to think more carefully about assessment;

- staff support for self-development – staff responses on this issue are quite revealing. All the staff and most of the students (67 per cent) felt that students' approaches to study were monitored on arrival on the course. Most of the students (71 per cent) and two-thirds of the staff agreed that the students had not read the handbook and did not understand the concept of self-development. Two-thirds of the staff, but only 25 per cent of the students believed that appropriate training was provided for those students who were unfamiliar with self-development.

  Only half the tutors reported that the content of their unit is based upon the students' learning needs analysis. Most felt that there was sufficient time on the course to use self-development rather than formal lectures, and that they do not give formal lectures. All of them reported that their 'lectures' consisted of providing learning resources to facilitate group-based learning. All the tutors felt that it was not easy to obtain the extra resources needed to support resource-based learning. Interestingly, just under a third felt that their colleagues did not understand the requirements of a self-development approach to teaching and preferred to lecture.

  The students' mostly felt (60 per cent) that the content of unit 'lectures' was not negotiated. They were split fairly equally over preference for formal lectures or group-based learning. Similarly they were split on the issue of whether self-development groups were a peripheral (42 per cent) or central (50 per cent) part of course delivery at Crewe;

- relevance to the workplace – all the staff reported the view that the skills learned in the self-development groups would be useful in the students' workplace. Of the students, nearly 88 per cent reported that the skills learned in their self-development were useful in their workplace.

Conclusions

It appears that our experience at Crewe of using self-development groups on the first year of the DMS does not differ too much from what might be predicted from the literature. The areas where it seems that further work may be needed are given below.

The Tutors' Role

We need to spell out more clearly the role which tutors can play in supporting the groups. Students are not seeing the tutors as a learning resource. This may be because they have not got to know their tutor's areas of expertise as some tutors do not teach their block until near the end of the first year.

The Students' Role

Some students do not seem to take the groups seriously and this bothers those who do. This may be an intractable problem, but it could be significant that half the students see the groups as peripheral in course delivery. The issue of the isolation of the groups from the cohort as a whole is something which we should address.

The Learning Process

In this area it seems likely that the conditions are not sufficiently geared to making the most of self-development groups. The students feel that they do not receive sufficient training to enable them to change their approach to learning, nor do they have sufficient space in which to experiment. Most of the students did not feel that unit content was negotiated and half felt that the reproducing approach was rewarded in assessments.

We should perhaps look again at the workload and assessment methods we use if we wish to enhance the role of the self-development group. Similarly we appear to need some staff development workshops on how best to use the self-development approach for course delivery.

As Entwistle and Ramsden (1983) suggest, if we wish our students to undertake self-development then they must adopt a meaning approach to study. Whilst the appropriate organizational context will not guarantee that this approach is adopted, we can be sure that if we provide an inappropriate context it will prevent such an approach being adopted.

References

Belbin, R M (1981) *Management Teams: Why they succeed or fail*, Oxford: Heinemann.

Boud, D (ed.) (1988) *Developing Student Autonomy in Learning*, 2nd Edn, London: Kogan Page.

Entwistle, N and Ramsden, P (1983) *Understanding Student Learning*, Beckenham: Croom Helm.

Fisher, R A (1987) 'Diploma in management studies through a self-development approach', DPSE dissertation for Lancashire Polytechnic.

Gibbs, G (1992) *Improving the Quality of Student Learning*, Bristol: Technical and Educational Services Limited.

Higgs, J (1988) 'Planning learning experiences to promote autonomous learning' in Boud (ed.) *op. cit.*

Honey, P (1989) *Manual of Management Workshops*, Peter Honey, 10 Linden Avenue, Maidenhead, Berks.

Honey, P and Mumford, A (1989) *The Manual of Learning Opportunities*, Peter Honey, 10 Linden Avenue, Maidenhead, Berks.

Meyer, J F H and Parsons, P (1989) 'Approaches to study and course perception using the Lancaster Inventory – a comparative study', *Studies in Higher Education*, 14, 2.

Pedler, M (1986) 'Developing within the organisation: experiences with management self-development groups', *Management Education and Development*, 17, 1.

Chapter Fourteen

Using Group-based Learning in Chemical Engineering Studies

G S Bainbridge

Introduction

This chapter describes the development of group-based learning in chemical engineering at the University of Teesside. The first year of the BEng course is discussed in detail and extension of the techniques to later years of this course and to other courses is covered briefly.

The BEng course has been subject to constant improvement since its inception in 1968. A radical change in 1977 involved the introduction of group-based learning for students and group-based teaching for staff in the first year of the course. A decade later this method had proved its worth and been extended to other years and other courses, although chemical engineering still remains the only division within the school of engineering to use this method.

The first-year course

In re-designing the course in 1977, the staff team were constrained by the existing requirements for professional accreditation by the Institution of Chemical Engineers as well as by the CNAA. Our aims included an intention to make the course as flexible as possible to cope with the variety of students' needs and to develop further the strong industrial links which had been built up in the formative years of the course. It was also important to relate a variety of seemingly separate studies into an integrated course and to develop a positive student commitment to their studies.

The introduction of group-based methods was seen as a means of achieving this latter purpose. An immediate and significant improvement in student performance was observed. It took several years, though, to prove that this was not a transient effect due to other causes, and that it could be maintained both throughout the later years of the course and with successive cohorts of students. A full analysis of the effect of the changes was made in 1981 and, as a result, the course was recognized by the RSA Capability for Education citation in the following year.

Once the methods had been fully established, and with proven success, the philosophy was extended to the second and final years of the BEng course in 1987 and also used in the MEng course established in 1992. The BEng course won an Esso Partnership Award in 1989, and has been the cornerstone of the award of Class 1 status to chemical engineering at Teesside by the Department of Education and Science.

An analysis in 1987 showed that the mean proportion of students failing the first year had fallen by 10 per cent when comparing the periods 1968/76 and 1977/86, while there had been a simultaneous increase in the mean proportion gaining upper seconds from the same cohorts. No significant change was seen in the other honours classifications.

The philosophy introduced in 1977 incorporated block teaching with an integrated problem-solving approach. A considerable amount of continuous assessment is now used, supplemented by open-book examinations at the end of the year. A substantial proportion of a student's mark is obtained via peer assessment derived from student groups of up to six people. A prize is sponsored by industry for the most successful student group at the end of the first year.

The students meet a variety of real problems of gradually increasing complexity throughout the year. This builds up their confidence in a discipline in which most of them have had no prior experience. It also achieves the objective of relating the course material to industrial situations using the integrated approach. Many local industrial colleagues have become closely involved with the presentation of the material.

This part of the course is intended to equip students with the necessary elementary skills and techniques of chemical engineering through the iterative study of one central problem at progressively more complex levels. This main problem is a study of one particular chemical process, such as the production of polyvinyl chloride (which was used in the initial course) or the manufacture of ammonia (which is in use currently). The process is chosen to ensure that all the information which the student may require is already relatively well documented. The problem is studied in three cycles, namely:

- a steady-state material balance;
- a steady-state material and energy balance;
- balances with chemical reaction.

In each case the cycle commences with an informative problem-appraisal session lasting several days. For this the students are encouraged to identify skills and techniques which they require in order to solve the main problem. The work includes literature surveys, plant visits and simple exercises aimed at identifying the skills and techniques which must be studied before the problem can be tackled with confidence. In effect the students identify their own curriculum for the immediate future.

After several weeks in which the material is taught using a flexible blend of lectures, tutorials and projects, the last week is devoted to the final solution to the main problem. After the first cycle the process begins over again by expanding the complexity of the problem to identify the need for further study. This is repeated to move from the second cycle to the third, at the end of which the students tackle their formal open-book examinations.

Some subjects must necessarily be covered outside this scheme since they cannot be entirely related to a particular process. Two examples are mathematics and chemistry: the latter must include recognition that there are other chemicals in addition to those associated with ammonia! A few hours in each week are therefore devoted to teaching in the traditional manner.

Extension to other courses

As stated earlier, the techniques have gradually been copied to other areas, namely the first year of the Higher National Diploma course, followed by the second year of the BEng course, then (in 1991) the final year of the BEng course – all in chemical engineering. The operation of the first year of the HND is very similar to that of the BEng, with the minor additional constraint of incorporating the BTEC modular format. In the second year of the BEng course various cycles of work are centred upon the study of particular units within a chemical process. In the final year this is extended or repeated at greater depth. These cycles are related to one another through the students' earlier first-year experience, together with their relevance in the major design project which all students must tackle (in groups) in their final year.

The BEng course has recently been extended, by one further academic session, to lead to an MEng award. The group-based learning approach has been adopted here from the outset and the curriculum is covered almost entirely through group activities. The final year of the BEng course is split into halves and spread over two academic sessions, leaving the remaining halves of each year to be filled with MEng material. This arrangement has also been adopted by the BEng course in instrumentation and control so that the MEng curriculum, and therefore its presentation, is common to both.

The backbone to this course is the use of the project clinic, a development unique in the UK, in which a team of students from several scientific and technological disciplines work on a live industrial project over a period of about eight months. The aims of each individual project are formulated in detail in consultation between academic supervisors and the industrial client and a fee is also negotiated. Participation in this activity is optional for BEng students but those electing to study for the MEng award must carry out one project as a member of a team with their BEng colleagues and then manage a second project in the following (final) session. The remainder of the MEng curriculum comprises detailed studies of areas of common interest to the participating disciplines, carried out in a similar fashion to the first year using a flexible combination of lectures, tutorials, seminars and case-studies.

Staff commitment

Because the courses are designed to be flexible in operation, the use of staff time needs to be equally fluid. For the first year a team comprising about six staff is formed (the exact number being dependent upon the number of students registered). The team leader is responsible for managing the use of the team throughout the academic session and the staff commitment is decided at regular meetings held weekly or fortnightly.

The expertise and number of staff required at any time depends upon the academic material and the chosen blend of lectures, tutorials and project work. On many occasions most or all members of the team may be needed to take part in general discussions or group feedback or presentation sessions. Membership of such a small dedicated staff team brings improved motivation and performance, but at the expense of a significant increase in staff time.

In the early days, with only the first-year course affected, handling things in this way was relatively easy, simply involving the need to recognize other regular staff commitments in an otherwise normal timetable. However, now that all teaching in chemical engineering is organized in this way there is no formal timetabling whatsoever, except for identifying the venue. Each member of staff may belong to three or even four different teams, each organized separately. Each staff member manages his or her own time, effectively contracting to provide service to a particular team on request in a negotiated time-slot.

If such a scheme were to be contemplated *ab initio* it would probably be rejected as ludicrous – but, having gradually developed to operating seven teams simultaneously we have shown that the philosophy is still working, and successfully too.

Chapter Fifteen

Learning Journals for Evaluation of Group-based Learning

Marjorie Talbot

Background

This chapter describes the use of learning contracts and learning journals on a multidisciplinary education programme in health visiting and nursing at the University of East London.

A brief excursion into the history of nursing education is particularly relevant here, in view of the prevailing culture built up over a long period of time, that now affects the way innovations such as group-based learning are integrated within the curriculum.

Nurses have traditionally been educated for a role in which they are seen as constantly attending the sick, under the direction of doctors and within a hospital setting (Nightingale, 1860, cited in Burnard and Chapman, 1990, p.4). Thus the pattern of nursing curricula has, until recently, stressed preparation for efficient task-doers assisting the doctor's orders. Nursing programmes have, in the main, been located in schools attached to hospitals, resulting in convergent thinking and instrumental training.

In contrast, education for post-registration education for health visitors and district nurses has always been located within higher education institutions and has emphasized the promotion of health for individuals and families in their homes, requiring greater initiative on the part of the carer. Health education and disease prevention have since become more clearly affirmed as key skills requiring particular interpersonal skills for health visitors and district nurses working alongside general medical practitioners and other professionals. The relatively recent emergence of the primary health care multidisciplinary team has recharged the debate on nurse education.

This chapter focuses on a learning contract for the negotiation of student-centred learning methods utilized for teaching health education and primary prevention to health visitors and nurses. The project has attempted to reorientate the curriculum process away from instrumental preparation for task-doers (Blaney, 1974, cited in Burnard and Chapman, 1990, p.41) and towards principles of negotiated learning within the syllabus. The practice of health education and primary prevention by health visitors and nurses can be described as the 'art of negotiated care'. Schön's classic paper (1983) on the reflective practitioner argues the attributes of 'intuitive artistry' found in the judgements of competent professional practice. He describes the conscious ability to evaluate, bringing meaning to performance of actions. This critical reflection upon practice provides the opportunity to recognize previously unexamined assumptions, leading to future learning and enhanced competence. It seems that Schön's reflective practitioner identifies desirable skills for negotiated care, especially in interdisciplinary team-work and inter-agency liaison health promotion. The development of competence to take responsibility for decision making in a multidisciplinary team requires prior opportunity to raise awareness of self.

Similarly group-work provides a strategy for student-centred learning, based on syllabus content, utilising Knowles' principles of personhood in experiential learning (Jarvis, 1984) and by community action (Brookfield, 1986, cited in Burnard and Chapman, 1990, p.45). The latter, in particular, draws attention to the ideas of collective activity in small groups, characterized by alternating action and reflection, ideas ideally mirrored in primary health care teams. These concepts of personhood, experiential learning and action-reflection form the perspective upon which learning contracts may be negotiated as a strategy for student-centred learning, within a formal curriculum process in primary health care.

What follows describes an initiative in curriculum development intended to increase student-centred learning. The project aims to develop skills of self-confidence and collaborative enterprise within the context of shared multidisciplinary learning in the fields of health education and primary prevention. The participants are student community psychiatric nurses, district nurses and health visitors on a full-time 52-week diploma course, comprising 71 course members and three teachers.

The learning contract

Learning contracts were introduced in order to increase the opportunity for students to negotiate their learning processes and resources within the constraints of the syllabus content and the overall course curriculum. The course is centrally concerned with post-basic professional education and therefore involves the interests of colleagues in the field and the general public. These latter two groups are represented by practice-teachers and managers of the employing agency. Health education and social aspects of health and disease are the two subjects addressed and evaluated.

For the first cohort involved in the process the idea of the learning contract was introduced in the second week of the course and the programme completed with tutor feedback on a written assignment towards the end of the year. After a classroom presentation on learning contracts students were informed on non-negotiable taught content and were given a timetabled structure providing classroom space and tutor availability for negotiated encounters when experiential learning might occur.

The cohort was organized into 12 small groups. Each group was allocated a topic to study from the 'Social aspects of health and disease' syllabus. A tutor identified for each topic was to act as consultant. Timetabled resources in the first term included six hours training on group-work skills and self-awareness, five hours training on teaching skills and audio-visual presentation, and 15 hours teaching on health promotion models and theories. Term two timetabling provided 39 hours of student-led discussion periods. Each group was allocated two hours for students' group-work presentations.

During the group-work training, the students and their project tutors collaborated to negotiate the evaluation criteria. This included a journal of their experiential learning encounters. At this stage, the assessment guidelines were also reviewed to include an appended copy of the journal. The groups were encouraged to have at least one meeting with their topic consultant and to negotiate further meetings according to their wishes. The project tutors were available on request, especially during timetabled student discussion periods. The presentation by each of the 12 groups, timetabled for the end of the second term, was to be held separately, attended by the topic specialist and by the students' practice-teacher.

The journal as a learning tool

A version of the journal has been used on the 'joint community practice teacher' course at the Institute of Health and Rehabilitation for several years, as part of continuous assessment in interdisciplinary professional development and curriculum studies. The mixed responses from this course over the years provided some useful background experiences on which to draw during the design of this project. It has been found, for example, that whether guidelines for completing a journal were given formally or negotiated on individual request made little difference to outcomes.

Our students appreciated hearing about the journal as a tool for self-evaluation, to focus learning on skills of reflecting upon action in group-work. The journal could also be seen to form the basis of an individual student-student discussion in their group, or as a tutor-student discussion on self-awareness in the area of group dynamics. The groups were encouraged to negotiate their own terms of utility and to consider confidentiality within the group. The matter of appending journal material to their assignment, in support of their evaluation of preparation for the health education presentation, was discussed at an early group-work workshop. Students gave a mixed response. Sensitive feelings about self-disclosure and also loyalty to fellow group members were considered, explored and followed up on request.

The process

The students seemed to launch themselves immediately into investigating their topic according to personal interest and without much thought beyond that of assessment. However, once the group-work workshops and taught sessions on health promotion had taken place a change came over most individuals towards a collective consciousness. Attempts were now made to forge group allegiances in order to negotiate a shared approach to the task. From this point forward activity was not easily observed over the next few weeks, other than some negotiated and some unexplained absences from the classroom! The time for group presentations arrived and brought a flurry of enthusiasm and demand for resources in the classrooms.

From my own experience and from reports by the topic tutors attending, the work presented was well researched and demonstrated considerable and coordinated effort. There was evidence of mutual awareness and cooperation and innovative rehearsal of gender and cultural differences between group members. Their sense of enterprise usually facilitated successful team building. It seemed that much more had been learned than might have been taught using conventional pedagogy.

Lessons to be learned

Several aspects of the project can be improved to further strengthen the advantages of using learning journals. The following comments are raised from the coordinators' observations.

The course members each participated in their group presentation and submitted a piece of work for assessment following the curriculum guidelines. However, the levels of enjoyment and sense of benefit varied within groups and between groups. This was similarly reflected among staff for whom there had, I believe, been inadequate training for facilitating group-work and student journals. Furthermore, there was some confusion between the assigned role of topic tutor and an assumed role of facilitator which had not been clearly established between the tutors or negotiated with the students.

The matter of tutor-facilitated student-centred study skills was inadequately addressed during the orientation programme for the course. The course cohort is large and, despite a personal tutorial system for meeting individual needs, there was clearly some difficulty experienced in staff-student monitoring regarding the maintenance of group-life in the context of this project. The outcome was that several students had a poor experience in their group, becoming isolated in pursuing independent learning rather than student-centred collaborative study.

Several students submitted a summative and reflective report on group-work but without the evidence of an accompanying contemporaneous journal. However, these students did demonstrate satisfactory understanding of the ideas of personhood, responsibility and accountability in group-work as it relates to health education.

The most successful group had found its own leader early in the process and negotiated for tutor assistance in relation to the topic, group-life maintenance and journals, and clarification on the negotiated guidelines for assessment. This group presented their material from the perspective of their audience interests. Peer participation was encouraged as a focus based upon thorough research. The individuals in this group demonstrated their confidence in submitting competent assignments complete with appended journals.

The post-course student questionnaire

A post-course questionnaire sought to evaluate student and staff experience of the unit programme and the extent to which learning was integrated into the period of supervised practice following the taught programme.

The questionnaire offered a series of closed questions about self-directed learning and the learning journal, followed by some statements drawing upon attitudes to group-work, to working in teams, to the journal as a learning strategy and to personal behaviour in inter-professional collaboration. The questionnaire was completed during attendance on the final week of the course, following completion of supervised practice.

While most students claimed to have enjoyed the course module overall, one third of the responses indicated no previous experience of self-directed learning. Two students who did not enjoy the module claimed to be experienced in self-directed learning. Six students disagreed with the notion that group-work is an enjoyable learning method. A few students claimed that their group-work facilitator was unavailable when needed. However it is not possible to know whether these latter responses are linked.

Negotiation of the learning contract had included the purpose and boundaries for keeping a process journal. While two-thirds of the cohort claimed in response to the questionnaire that they had engaged in a learning contract and valued keeping a learning journal, there were two who disclaimed the learning contract and five who contradicted themselves as to whether they thought they had agreed to keeping a contemporaneous diary to support a critical account of their group-work dynamics. There are indications of small numbers of disaffected students, but it is difficult to know at this early stage whether they should act as a warning. Their failure to engage in the process brings into question the notion of the value of a learning journal, for example, in helping students build reflective competence in confronting fear associated with peer evaluation in group-work and team building. Indeed four student health visitors and two district nurses claimed not to value the journal as a learning method; however only one of these stated that the journal had not been helpful in reflective competence and each agreed upon the importance of self-awareness in collaborative practice.

Group-work is held to be a strategy for building confidence and empowering its members in developing and using interpersonal skills. These skills are significant in both the practice of health education and also in interdisciplinary collaboration. As there is increasing attention in the field to inter-agency and inter-sectoral collaboration in health promotion and primary health care, it was the intention of the project team that competence for such practice be developed. All except three of the respondents claimed to be better able to work with others in inter-professional activity as a result of their experience. Two-thirds said they strongly preferred an identified team leader. Nine students felt that their course-work experience in group-work had reflected a mirror image of practice relationships. A few students agreed that they still prefer to work alone as much as possible.

It seems that these responses reflect something of the acceptance of interdisciplinary educational strategies as being congruent with expectations in practice. However, along with this there is perhaps an awareness of the turbulence experienced in current organizational change, bringing the need for clear management leadership.

The post-course staff questionnaire

The staff who facilitated the group-work and supervised teaching presentations were also invited to complete a questionnaire. This focused on three areas: group-work as a learning strategy; the need for competent facilitation of the learning contract in order to achieve goals; and the use by students of a learning journal as a strategy for strengthening reflective thinking on the group dynamics.

Further comments were also invited. Responses were received from four of the five original facilitator team, one member having retired from the department. There was an overall positive belief in the utility of group-work in this context together with the need for a competent facilitator. Each lecturer agreed that a learning journal is important in developing reflective competence for collaborative practice although there was little commitment in their responses to recognition of the learning contract. One lecturer was unconvinced of the importance of involving the student's clinical teacher in their placement, whilst another responded from the firm belief that this course unit reflects the health promotion experiences found in community practice, and serves to develop a set of values shared by student and clinical teacher.

Concluding remarks

In summary, this curriculum development project has enabled us to study our teaching methods. We have designed ways of improving the autonomy of our students on this professional course, and to negotiate their experiential learning in transferable skills in health promotion. The evaluation has illuminated some aspects of satisfaction and success based on our negotiated goals for both students and staff.

However, we have also discovered some difficulties. These are largely concerned with the nature of the learning contract and what it means to be a facilitator in higher education. It seems that some students resented the responsibility to individually engage in a learning contract and tutors may not fully understand the method as a means to facilitating group-work. The matter of acting as a facilitator and as a topic specialist tutor contributed to some confusion for staff in terms of how they used time spent within the group. These matters have now become visible to the course team and may be included in our staff development programme. Overall it has been an illuminating project, enabling staff to facilitate the development of student competencies.

References

Burnard, P and Chapman, C (1990) *Nurse Education: The Way Forward*, Harrow: Scutari Press.

Jarvis, P (1984) *Professional Education*, Beckenham: Croom Helm.

Schön, Donald A (1983) *The Reflective Practitioner*, New York: Basic Books.

Schön, Donald A (1987) 'The crisis of professional knowledge', *Journal of Interprofessional Care*, 6, 1, 1992,49–63.

Chapter Sixteen

Working in Groups and Teams
Jim McNally

Introduction

Within higher education we are increasingly exhorted to promote group-based learning. It is worth looking closely both at the stated purposes and expected benefits; thereafter, it is worth identifying the possible constraints and means of countering them.

The purposes of group-work

Proposals to extend group- and team-working cite the following as their main purposes in using these methods:

- students working in groups and teams have, in each other, additional means of learning support and formative assessment. For example, by the division of labour, groups can generate a greater sum of knowledge than can an individual; and after informed discussion the knowledge available to the group may be greater than the sum of individual contrbutions;
- projects based on group- and team-work will almost certainly be focused on active and student-centred learning, with clear benefits in understanding and retention of subject-specific knowledge and skills;

- the need for communication and information skills helps develop expertise which will be transferable to employment roles and tasks, thus 'adding value' to graduates beyond their disciplinary expertise;
- more complex group-projects provide opportunities to develop the 'higher order' qualities increasingly expected of graduates destined for the 'fast track'. In particular, such graduates are looked on as a latent source of capability in decision making, problem solving and conflict resolution;
- through using groups it becomes feasible to undertake meaningful projects for external organizations with benefits for all parties. For example, employers may provide educational inputs, offer stimulating learning processes to students, and all parties may gain beneficial outputs (research findings, prototypes, piloted questionnaires and so on).

The benefits of group-work

Notwithstanding the purposes, are additions to the curriculum such as group-work really necessary when most higher education institutions provide tutorials and seminars? A brief look at recent research findings indicates that additional opportunities for working in groups and teams are indeed very necessary.

Table 16.1 (at the end of this chapter) shows that graduates consider that during their time in higher education they particularly developed those skills mainly used in isolation, such as critical thought and independence. However, graduates could benefit by further developing those qualities which require interaction with others such as cooperation, political consciousness and leadership.

Perhaps these relative shortcomings in developing the skills of working with others can be traced to staff whose approach is founded on the transmission of subject-specific knowledge. Some staff take every opportunity of silence in tutorials or seminars to switch to lecture mode, to the undoubted delight of students more at ease in a passive educational role.

Two studies of small group teaching quoted by Brown and Atkins (1988) are particularly revealing on this issue, finding that:

- tutor talk reached 86 per cent of time spent;
- student interaction could be as low as 8 per cent;
- tutor used student ideas less than 2 per cent of the time;
- lecturing in small groups varied from 7 to 70 per cent of the time;
- asking questions varied from 1 to 28 per cent of the time;
- mean time spent talking by tutors was 64 per cent.

These findings also indicate that even critical and independent thinking could be further enhanced by more interaction in tutorials and seminars.

The value to graduates of acquiring skills and knowledge beyond those developed within their discipline clearly needs to be more fully promoted. Justification can be found in the figures in Table 16.2 at the end of this chapter. The figures here show that in 1990 the majority of graduates sampled were recruited for expertise outside their discipline-specific skills and knowledge.

An indication of what employers are looking for is given in Table 16.3. Many of the characteristics ranked here as 'most significant' are clearly those which ensure effectiveness in working with others, as opposed to those needed by individuals working in isolation.

The constraints of group-work

Several constraints work so as to inhibit the extension of group-work in higher education. Constraints cited by staff include: there is insufficient time to 'cover the subject'; staff feel less in control of learning; students like being teacher-dependent; and staff do not possess the necessary skills to implement this approach. Additional staff development, more adequate resourcing, new forms of assessment and dialogue with external bodies are ideas which could help in extending the use of group-work.

However, a more fundamental concern is the lack of reference by exponents of group-work to research and theory in the field. This omission, if not countered, might inhibit conversion to and conviction in the use of group-based learning. This absence of explicit references to theory and research is likely to have its roots in the assumption that groups have a clear and unchallenged role in enhancing creativity, with benefits for problem solving, decision making and conflict resolution. In reality, doubt has long been cast on this fundamental assumption.

In *The Art of the Soluble* Medawar (1967) put his view succinctly:

having an idea or framing a hypothesis is an imaginative exploit of some kind, the work of a single mind; obviously trying it out must be a ruthlessly critical process to which many skills and many hands may contribute.

More recent empirical work on brainstorming supports Medawar's speculation. Adrian Furnham of the Business Psychology Unit at UCL very lucidly summarized the significant research in a recent issue of *New Scientist*:

comparisons were made of the number of ideas/issues/outcomes generated by groups of four or seven people and a like number of individuals working on the same problem alone. Individuals were far more productive than groups and arrived at their solutions much faster (Furnham, 1994).

Interestingly, as suggested by Medawar, Furnham also notes that,

research indicates that groups performing well-structured tasks tend to make better, more accurate decisions but take more time to reach them than individuals ... the average accuracy of groups of five was greater than the average accuracy of five individuals working alone.

In an oral communication, Professor Furnham agreed that it is likely to be insufficient only to establish rules and regulations for group operation: training, based on research findings, in the forms of behaviour which contribute to success and failure must be appreciated, acquired and practised.

Conclusions

There is a clear need to promote group- and team-work as an invaluable opportunity to gain those transferable skills, so clearly sought in graduates (oral communication, leading and motivating, team-work), which will not be fostered in traditional forms of education where isolation and inhibition are the narrow diet provided in lectures and libraries.

A balanced educational diet must be offered. The evidence above suggests that without a commitment to group-work, seminars and tutorials will not be an adequate alternative. Further, as student numbers grow and educational technology is used to aid expansion, the need for effective and efficient group-work can no longer be left to committed staff or possible spontaneity in seminars (which are in any case becoming less available to students as numbers rise).

A variety of approaches to group-work and the benefits to be gained from them can be seen in the following examples of Enterprise in Higher Education projects at Glasgow University.

Tribunal Representation

Undergraduate law students are trained by 'Citizens' Advice Scotland' to undertake representation work in local bureaux. The training period is four weeks; thereafter, the students are required to work three to four hours per week in a local bureau. This project is particularly beneficial in developing students' communication skills with people who know less than they do. This is important as, in education, students are used to listening to, speaking with, and writing for academic staff who know more about the subject studied, whereas after graduating, lawyers' most crucial communication will be with people who know less than they do: clients and jurors.

Medieval History Tutorials

In one class tutorials now operate as formal meetings with a chairperson and minute-taker, roles which all students must undertake over the course. Open learning material is used to promote the idea as worthwhile in adding to students' expertise and to support student performance in the roles to be filled in meetings.

Training for Class Representatives

The need for class representatives is heavily publicized and training courses are offered to students on campus and in halls of residence. Initial feedback from staff is that current class representatives are more committed and effective than their predecessors.

Group-Work in Mathematics

This project is showing clearly that even a subject thought to require a highly individualistic mode of study is suitable for group-work. Mathematics problems are given which are amenable to partial solutions by individuals who then as a group pool their findings in order to solve the larger problems. One purpose behind this project is to help develop mathematicians who can understand other perspectives, grasp new ideas, and add their exactness to mixed-discipline groups charged with tasks which require a mix of rigour and creativity, for example traffic management.

Finally, Lagowski's work, encapsulated in Table 16.4, suggests that student retention is best supported in subject-specific and transferable expertise by ensuring that teaching, learning and assessment are founded on students saying and doing something about what they are thinking, and not just saying it to themselves.

References

Brennan, J and McGeevor, P (1988) *Graduates at Work*, London: Kingsley.

Brown, G and Atkins, M (1988) *Effective Teaching in Higher Education*, London: Methuen.

Furnham, A (1994) 'When change is s-shaped' in *New Scientist*, **141**, 1908, 46–7.

Medawar, P (1967) 'Two Conceptions of Science', in *The Art of the Soluble*, London: Methuen.

Graduate perception of the benefits of higher education (2 years after graduation) where great improvement = 100; and no improvement = 0

critical thinking	79
independence	75
organization	75
writing ability	68
applying knowledge	67
confidence	67
understanding others	64
logical thought	64
speaking ability	58
cooperation	58
responsibility	56
numeracy	48
political consciousness	42
leadership	39

Table 16.1 *The benefits of higher education*
Source: Brennan and McGeevor (1988)

Vacancies for graduates of 'any discipline'			
Year	Total no. of vacancies	'Any discipline' no. of vacancies	'Any discipline' per cent of vacancies
1980	7731	2431	31.4
1990	12,314	6568	53.3

Table 16.2 *Graduate vacancies*
Source: Current Vacancies, Central Services Unit

Ranked, 1 = most significant	
1. Oral communication	10. Foreign language competence
2. Teamwork	11. Energetic
3. Enthusiasm	12. Innovative
4. Motivation	13. Ambitious
5. Initiative	14. Managing
6. Leadership	15. Drive
7. Commitment	16. Dynamic
8. Interpersonal	17. Determination
9. Organizing	

Table 16.3 *Characteristics significant to recruiters*
Source: Personal Skills Unit, Sheffield University, 1991

Students retain:

10 per cent	of what they read
26 per cent	of what they hear
30 per cent	of what they see
50 per cent	of what they see and hear
70 per cent	of what they say
90 per cent	of what they say as they do something

Table 16.4 *Rentention rates for student learning*
Source: Lagowski (1990) *Journal of Chemical Education* 67, 811.

Case Studies Involving Group-work

Through description of a number of case studies from different disciplines, this section illustrates the way group-based learning can be used for a wide variety of purposes. Purposes range here from the understanding of subject-matter, through the acquisition of technical and personal skills, to increasing motivation.

An example of a group-project with a highly task-orientated structure is described by Pressnell at the University of Hertfordshire. Students are assigned task-related roles within the project, and in addition to the technical issues of the design task the experience of group dynamics is also seen as an important aim.

Grant at Leicester University makes an interesting comparison between two Enterprise case studies. In both cases there is a strong emphasis on learning group and interpersonal skills. The progress of the two projects demonstrates the effect that a discipline's existing culture has on the outcome when introducing a specific learning method.

Harris, Bramhall and Robinson at Sheffield Hallam University report on a case-study used to promote the integration of discipline material on an integrated engineering course. Groups of students form a 'ghost company', operating at more senior levels as their course progresses, within a 'real-life' scenario.

Another case study from Leicester University, described by McHardy and Henderson, involves a business game. Called 'Management indecision', this game has been specially designed to encourage creativity, and is based on a knowledge/skills model of learning. The game environment requires the use of the 'taught' elements of the course in creative and intuitive ways, and through which the knowledge and skills elements are integrated. This particular case study also provides a good example of the way a course team can undertake curriculum development in a truly group-based way.

At the University of Hertfordshire Shah uses group-work to help pre-pare student history teachers for the role of subject coordinators. The complexity of the requirements for teacher education, well illustrated here, make group-work a particularly appropriate method.

Chapter Seventeen

A Case Study of a Group-project in Aerospace Design Engineering

Martyn S Pressnell

Introduction

As the culmination of three years of study towards the BEng in aerospace engineering, students undertake a group aircraft design study. During this project students find that the difficulty of problems associated with group dynamics rivals that of the technical problems of aircraft design.

The course aims to simulate the situation which occurs in industry during the early stages of a new aircraft design. At that time there will be relatively few engineers involved, but they will have a good deal of experience. Political and economic factors will invariably be present and will tend to produce obstacles only overcome by the most persistent design organization.

Organization of the project

The task specified for the project is topical, in that it is one of the most critical issues currently facing the aerospace industry, namely the regional airliner. About 100 students operate in groups of five or six. Their work is largely self-directed, with staff acting in a consultative or advisory role. The project represents one module of student work.

It is recognized that students will not be able to fully design, or even fully specify, an aircraft in the time available. The intention is that they will sample the design experience and go as far as time and other constraints permit.

The work requirement for each student designer is individually defined. Each student is expected to work as a collaborative partner within his or her team, to face the technical issues together, and to share the decision taking. The student team leader, responsible for organization and management, plays a unique role in promoting the harmony of the team and must be elected by the group with some care.

Students are assigned to groups in a random order. Each group must nominate all individuals to group roles by the end of the first day of project work. Roles are specified as group leader and designers for five aircraft sections, namely wing, fuselage, tail unit, engine installation and undercarriage. Responsibilities for these roles are specified in some detail in the project brief.

A member of staff is attached to each project group, in accordance with a five-week rota. It may be that a group wanting to do aerodynamics work will have a supervisor expert in structural design. It would then be important that the group makes full use of the advice immediately available, while ensuring that some group members pursue aerodynamics by self-directed reading and research. In other words, the group must forward plan and not be thrown into disarray by events. This situation is reflected in industry, where projects are managed to facilitate the interplay of all disciplines. Indeed, there is no step-by-step sequence by which the task will logically be accomplished. It will be helpful to take arbitrary decisions from time to time in order that work can proceed, even if ultimately the decision proves second best.

The design groups are expected to imagine that they represent an international consortium of manufacturers, with the necessary financial capacity to launch a new aircraft. They will need to study competitive machines, but may not simply produce another airliner of similar capability. For marketing reasons their solution must be modern and distinctive in style, ahead of, or certainly at, the 'state of the art'.

The project is timetabled to operate for three hours per week. There are 16 student groups, tutored by eight academic staff. There is also librarian support. Each member of academic staff supervises two groups at the rate of one hour per week per group. This cycles through a rota, so that each staff member handles eight groups in total. The programme is divided into four phases of supervision, the last week of which will be for staff/peer assessment of each student's effort. The course concludes with submission of portfolios of work and group presentations.

During supervision, staff will act in the role of consultant. It is the responsibility of the group, acting under the general direction of their chosen leader, to maximize this consultancy opportunity. Emphasis will be on the group leader to organize and manage their group's effort, with the guidance of staff as required.

Assessment

Marks come from four individual phase assessments of 12 per cent each, (ie, 48 per cent), a group presentation (22 per cent) and an individual portfolio of work (30 per cent). The emphasis is on team activity, and the assessment reflects this throughout.

In the four phases there is a strong element of peer assessment, each group member being required to complete an assessment of each of his or her peers in the group, using a phase assessment proforma. The individual assessment is then discussed between the leader of the group and the supervisor, in private consultation. The supervisor meets with the whole group to receive general comments, and to ask pertinent questions of individuals. Finally, the supervisor discusses the work of the leader in his · or her absence. The supervisor moderates and awards the marks as judged appropriate, completing the staff assessment form, which is similar to the students' form. Grades are published after the second and fourth phases, using the letter grades A (excellent) to F (fail).

The actual presentation of the group's work is made by the leader, with contributions from some or all of the other members, as the group decides. The time allowed is 40 minutes, after which an overall assessment is made jointly by the supervisors present. The group is awarded a joint mark, each member being equally rewarded. However, in exceptional circumstances, if a member plays no part in the preparation or presentation, or is absent from the proceedings for no good reason, a zero mark may be recorded. The portfolio of individual work is a collection of the work undertaken, suitably indexed and introduced. Portfolios are assessed by a panel of supervisors. Typically the portfolio should contain:

- a summary of work undertaken. The leader of a group should also include a summary of the organizational aspects of work specific to the role of leader. Others may comment on working as part of a team;
- general aspects of the aircraft designed, any work relevant to the individual role being specially identified. Common material such as specifications and drawings;
- a summary of calculations undertaken, with the results presented as graphs, or tables;
- drawings to show the layout of specific components assigned to the individual role. Schematic drawings and details as defined for the particular designer;

- a description of common policies adopted, including the methods of manufacture. In the case of the leader, a market strategy.

Chapter Eighteen

Group-project Work: Two Enterprise Case Studies

Annie Grant

Background

The Enterprise in Higher Education Initiative (EHE) is currently an important agent for change in the higher education sector, particularly in the area of teaching and learning. A common feature of all EHE programmes is that they provide a stimulus to academic staff to develop or enhance teaching and learning styles that are specifically directed to facilitating students' acquisition of personal transferable skills, particularly those that have relevance to employment.

Although the skills highlighted in individual EHE programmes vary, they tend to include effective communication, problem solving abilities, numeracy and computer literacy, self-awareness, decisiveness and leadership. Most lists of relevant skills will also include the ability to work independently and the ability to work in collaboration with others. Traditionally, higher education has placed a great deal of emphasis on the former, and assessment methods have been geared to, if not driven by, a perceived imperative to assess individual achievement, and to preclude the possibility of collaboration or collusion. However, in the world of work team-work is normal, and broader and flatter collaborative management structures are increasingly common (Bartol and Martin, 1991, pp. 550–51). In Green's analysis of advertisements for graduate-level posts, the ability to work effectively in teams was ranked second (with oral communication first) as the personal skill most frequently mentioned (Green, 1990).

Academic research, particularly in the sciences but also in other disciplines, often involves a substantial degree of collaboration or team-work. It is not clear whether it is specifically the EHE initiative, or a more general perception of changes in the demands of employers, or indeed academic research practice that has had the most effect in stimulating an interest in the development of opportunities for students to develop team-working skills, but there is undoubtedly a growing interest in the introduction of course elements that move the emphasis from the performance of the individual as an individual to the performance of the individual within a group.

This chapter discusses group project work that has been introduced as a course element in two departments at the University of Leicester: the Department of Physics and Astronomy and the School of Archaeological Studies. It then looks at some of the issues that have emerged as a result of these changes to traditional teaching and learning, comparing and contrasting the experiences of two rather different subjects and departments.

Group-work in the physics department

Physics teaching in higher education has recently been the subject of a detailed investigation by a working party of the Institute of Physics, the Standing Conference of Physics Professors and the Committee of Heads of Physics in Polytechnics. Their report recommended that the content of single honours physics degree courses should be substantially reduced but that it should be taught in such a way that 'the students achieved a markedly fuller understanding of the subject, and had more opportunity to develop the relevant skills'. Skills in collaboration and communication were highlighted in the report, and project work was also identified as important.

The Physics and Astronomy Department at Leicester University has responded to the challenge of teaching physics in the 1990s and the opportunities for funding provided by the EHE initiative with a review of its teaching, one outcome of which was an 'Enterprise plan' which identified a series of aims and objectives for physics students that included the ability to work in a group, organize a group activity and prepare a joint report. In order to achieve these aims, group-project work was introduced into the second year undergraduate curriculum for the first time during the 1991/2 academic year.

The specific aims of the group-projects were identified by the department as being:

- to develop group skills;
- to use physics-based knowledge in a non-academic context; to reinforce this knowledge and to appreciate the requirements for 'robust knowledge';
- to develop communication and presentation skills; and
- to appreciate time and resource management.

The 1991/2 second year consisted of 75 students, who were divided into ten groups and each allocated a topic. Topics included designing a travelling exhibition to illustrate the benefits of space research, writing a teachers' handbook to support the teaching of astronomy in primary schools, and making a ten-minute video on the solar system. Eight afternoons, over a ten-day period, were allocated to complete the task, and rooms were booked for students to use to meet and work in. The assessment for this course is 2 per cent of the final degree mark.

Group-work in the School of Archaeological Studies

The School of Archaeological Studies first introduced group-work into its second-year undergraduate course in 1989. The catalyst for this change in teaching practice was almost certainly the EHE initiative. However, two other factors were also important. Practical archaeology almost always involves team-work, and so the ability to work together is seen by most staff in the school as an essential skill for the discipline. The particular form of group-work chosen was stimulated by the introduction of the National Curriculum. The shortage of imaginative and up-to-date material for teachers to use for teaching some aspects of the new curriculum was brought to the attention of the school by the Leicestershire Education Authority advisory teacher for the humanities. The 'Schools project' as it is known, is a compulsory element of the course for second-year archaeology and archaeology/history students.

Groups of three or four students are allocated a supervisor and a topic and are given the task of producing a teaching and learning pack for pupils and teachers to tie in with specific elements of key stages two or three of the National Curriculum for history, geography or science. The range of topics that have been developed in this way is now very wide, and includes aspects of archaeology that reflect its links with science (for example, 'mining in the past', 'science before the Romans') as well as more obviously archaeological and historical topics (for example, 'Roman mosaics', 'standing building', 'Anglo-Saxon money').

The project is carried out in the students' own time, over two terms. The students themselves have to arrange meetings with their supervisor, with a norm of four to six hours suggested; there are no facilities provided for meeting as a group on any other occasion, thus they must arrange to do this in common rooms, canteens, bars or student lodgings. They are allocated a budget for materials and they are told that if they exceed this they may have marks deducted. The assessment for this course is 9 per cent of the final degree mark.

The two projects compared

There are differences in the project work set by the two departments in, for example, the nature of the tasks, group size, the length and magnitude of the tasks allotted, and the weight attached to the project work in the final degree assessment. There are also many important similarities that raise general issues relating to both the benefits and the problems of group-work, and how these latter might be addressed.

Forming Groups and Allocating Topics

One such issue relates to the initial setting-up procedures. In both departments the project titles were suggested by the members of staff who had agreed to act as project supervisors, and a final list, with no redundancies, was decided on by the course leaders.

The Physics Department (which introduced project work for the first time in 1992) gave each student a list of the topics and asked them to rate them in order of preference. The topics were then placed in order of popularity; students who had given the highest rating to the least popular topic were allocated this topic first and so on, until all students had been placed. In practice no student had to tackle a topic other than their first, second or third choice. Fortunately, the groups were well balanced in terms of ability and motivation. This method seems to have been successful, and staff felt that group dynamics had developed well over the ten days of the course.

There has been much discussion about the best methods to use for allocating students to groups and project topic in the Archaeology Department (which has just started the fourth year of their 'Schools project') and several different methods have been tried. An entirely random allocation of students both to group and topic led to a number of complaints. Some students said that the lack of enthusiasm they felt for their topic had adversely affected their work; others complained about the attitudes and commitment of their group members. However, there was also positive feedback about the benefits of being made to study a subject that was not expected to be interesting, and one student commented that developing the ability to work on any topic would be useful in the real world.

In several instances, where there were severe problems with group cohesion, the supervisor had to intervene to help the group to resolve them. In a subsequent year, the department enlisted the help of a student counsellor who facilitated the formation of groups by helping students to try to identify their own behaviour in a group situation. Groups were then formed with a balanced mix of personalities, and they were given some choice in their topic. This approach resolved some of the problems, although the support of supervisors in holding groups together was still needed occasionally.

In 1992, the student counsellor was ill and not able to help. By default, the students were given a much greater choice of both their partners and their topic. It will be interesting to see what effect this has: the member of staff who runs the course has expressed some regret as, for him, and for other members of staff, learning how to work with people that you may not like, or who have different attitudes or motivation, is a very important aspect of the course.

The Physics Department has experienced far fewer problems with group dynamics than the School of Archaeological Studies, and while this may be in part due to the longer experience of archaeology, it may also reflect other differences. Important factors may be group size (eight in contrast to four), and particularly the much shorter span over which the groups have to maintain themselves for the physics projects (ten days rather than two terms).

There are also other more practical differences which may be important. Physics students are provided with a meeting space, but this resource is not available in the Archaeology Department. The situation in archaeology is also exacerbated by differences in the timetable of students in the same groups; difficulty in arranging meeting times was seen as the greatest disadvantage of group-work in a questionnaire response. Both departments give students clear briefings at the beginning of the course; in archaeology this is spread over several sessions and includes information about the National Curriculum and guidelines for project planning.

Staff and Student Attitudes

In both departments there were differing levels of enthusiasm about the introduction of group-work amongst the staff, with, in some instances, some barely disguised hostility at the beginning. However, almost half the staff in the Physics Department and all the full-time and most of the part-time staff of the Archaeology Department are now enthusiastically involved. The high quality of the work produced by students has won over many of the doubters. The consistently positive response of the external examiners to the archaeology projects has also been an important factor in changing staff attitudes.

There has inevitably been a range of responses from the students themselves, who are frequently more conservative than staff about educational innovation. A questionnaire evaluation of the 1992/3 'Schools projects' revealed that students tend to split in two groups in their responses, either very positive or negative, with few falling between these two extremes. Several students identified specific difficulties in learning to work as a group, in defining goals, meeting agreed targets and managing time, and a significant proportion of the students encountered problems in ensuring an equal and fair workload among the members of the group. However, this evaluation was made during the course, and students tend to be more positive about the experience once they have completed the task.

An 'exit poll' the previous year suggested that many students felt that they had developed their appreciation, understanding and tolerance of others, together with their understanding of their own ability to cooperate with others. Almost all students said that they would like to have more project-based courses, although some added the proviso that this would be the case only if they were able to choose their own groups, or do individual project work.

Student responses to the physics and astronomy projects were by and large positive. A feature that the staff had not expected was that most of the groups became highly competitive, putting much more time and effort into the projects than had been envisaged. This caused no special difficulty when it was only a case of working during evenings and weekends, but some students also worked during mornings when they should have been attending lectures. The main criticisms of the project were of the assessment procedures, which are discussed below. Some of the negative responses of archaeology students were not encountered. Again, this may be because the time span for the physics projects was very much shorter.

Assessment

In both departments, the mark obtained for the project work contributes to the final degree class, although in the physics degree it is only a very small element. Many academic staff are hostile to group projects because of the assessment implications. Where a group activity is not in itself formally assessed, as might be the case in, for example, field work, staff are supportive of the activity for its own sake. However, plans for formally assessed group-project work can engender heated debates in staff meetings. Both departments have weathered, or averted, this problem and have independently chosen similar approaches.

In archaeology, the students are asked to hand in their project together with a set of supporting documents. These are one-page statements of the group aims and objectives, and a set of two-page 'diaries' or accounts by each student of their contribution to the project. The project is assessed by the examiners, who include the LEA humanities advisory teacher, and given a mark which is added to that awarded for a brief oral presentation by the group to the examiners. Where all the evidence (the group statement, the individual diaries, the oral presentation and the supervisor's opinion) suggests an equal contribution by all, the project mark is given to each of the contributors. Where this is not the case, individual marks are adjusted up or down from the project mark. Students who have not taken on a fair share of the work are penalized, and so are those who have worked hard but independently rather than cooperatively.

The physics projects are accompanied by a single page, agreed by the group, which is a statement of the contribution of each student. The individual marks combine the group mark given for the project, with an individual mark which takes into account the statement, the assessment of each individual by the supervisor, and each individual's performance when questioned orally by two staff members not otherwise involved in the project. The oral element is seen as an integral part of the course, and staff have commented on the students' articulate and effective defence of their work under cross-examination.

Both departments feel that they have arrived at solutions to the group assessment dilemma that are generally satisfactory, although these are reviewed and adjustments made each year. Archaeology was unhappy about their original method of assessment of the oral presentations, so last year both staff and students were given a detailed breakdown of the assessment criteria for the oral session. Students are also given full details of the assessment criteria for the projects at the beginning of the course.

Student criticisms of the physics and astronomy course were mainly of the assessment procedures, as many felt that their individual contributions had been insufficiently rewarded. Staff running the course are trying to improve the marking system by introducing a greater component of peer assessment, and by reducing the significance attached to the supervisors' assessments of individual performance, as this was felt to be rather subjective in some cases. There is, however, a concern that if too much attention is given to the individual marks, group dynamics may be adversely affected. In an internal report on the project for the Enterprise Office, the course leader commented that,

it is not even clear that one should worry too much about this: perhaps one of the things one learns from group-work is that the overall result is greater than the sum of the individual contributions, and that an 'enterprise culture' can produce a sharing of the benefits.

Conclusions

The group-project work set by both departments requires students to move beyond the strictly academic confines of their subject areas and attempt to communicate their subjects to the non-specialist. In the case of physics, this was clearly signalled in the aims and objectives for the group-work. Although the aims of the archaeology projects have not been stated in quite the same detail, those defined for the physics project could be seen to be entirely applicable to the 'Schools projects'.

This is a very important aspect of both projects and accounts in some significant measure for their success. By shifting the focus of the project work away from the narrowly academic, students are given the freedom to use the knowledge that they have acquired, and to take control, contribute their own ideas and develop their creativity. The mutual support and stimulation of the group can play an important part in this, and also make it possible to carry ideas through to the production stage in a relatively short space of time. Group projects that have a more narrowly academic focus have certainly been successful within their terms of reference, but they have frequently required greater input and control from supervisors and have not allowed the same opportunities for students to demonstrate their creativity.

The group-projects described have not only been instrumental in the development of team-working skills, but have provided opportunities for students to develop almost all the other personal skills listed at the beginning of this chapter. There is also a feeling amongst archaeology staff that participation in group-project work is a maturing experience for the students, and that they seem to perform better in their third-year courses as a result.

In such a brief account it has only been possible to raise a few of the issues arising from the experiences of these two departments, and discussion of these issues has perhaps raised as many new questions as it has answered. It is, however, clear that both courses are considered by their respective departments to be very successful and worthwhile. They will be continued and further developed in the future.

Both courses have also attracted favourable attention from outside the departments and the institution: school teachers have reacted very positively to some of the 'Schools projects' and to the astronomy syllabus. Two students groups in the School of Archaeological Studies and two in the Physics and Astronomy Department have won institutional prizes, and a submission from the Enterprise Unit on behalf of both departments has been rewarded in a national competition.

Acknowledgements: I should like to acknowledge the contribution made to this chapter by the staff and students involved, and in particular to thank Dr Derek Raine and Dr Alan Howe of the Department of Physics and Astronomy, and Professor Graeme Barker and Mr Paul Beavitt of the School of Archaeological Studies.

References

Bartol, K M and Martin, D C (1991) *Management*, New York: McGraw Hill.

Green, S (1990) *Analysis of Transferable Personal Skills Requested by Employers in Graduate Recruitment Advertisements in June 1989*, Personal Skills Unit, University of Sheffield.

Chapter Nineteen

Development of Group Skills using a Linked Assignment

R G Harris, M D Bramhall and I M Robinson

Introduction

Sheffield Hallam University was one of only six universities selected by the Engineering Council for support from the Department of Trade and Industry to develop pilot schemes leading to the award of new generalist engineering degrees. Each scheme was selected to emphasize different teaching and pedagogic innovations.

At Sheffield Hallam, the key theme for the new four-year sandwich degree in integrated engineering was developed around the concept of a 'ghost company' (Bramhall *et al.*, 1991). This is an imaginary company, having a well-documented history of some five years in the manufacture of components for the motor industry.

Students join the company as junior engineering staff when they enrol upon the degree course. As they progress through their studies, they are expected to adopt more responsible positions within the company; indeed, two have already been appointed to the board of directors. The board additionally comprises members of the course team, chaired on a part-time basis by a senior industrialist who gives approximately one week each year to inject a realistic business perspective to the company.

Course assignments

All the students undertake approximately 15 integrative assignments within the company during the course. The assignments provide a framework within which technical and business issues can be addressed. In addition, students are given encouragement and guidance in the development of personal skills. Each assignment has thus been carefully mapped out to ensure an even balance of subject material, to provide key integrative links into the ghost company scenario, and to provide opportunity for the development of appropriate personal skills. Approximately 60 per cent of the assignments are group-based, to encourage group and team synergy to develop.

Assessment in all assignments makes use of input from staff, the students themselves and their peers. For each assignment every student is required to present both a technical report and a short individual report. The individual report describes the process in which the solution was derived, assesses the dynamics of group operation, and evaluates the group and individual contributions.

Students also present a portfolio of their personal, professional and technical development over the period of the course. They are supported by the use of workbooks in which they log and record items and achievements of particular note throughout the course (Payne *et al.*, 1992). Students record evidence to ensure that material is available for the final portfolio presentation. The portfolio contributes 25 per cent towards final degree classification.

A novel feature of the programme, the 'linked assignments', involves students forming cross-cohort project teams. The more senior students in the course assume a more responsible role within the activity. One such linked assignment, the 'Design and construct' project undertaken by both first- and second-year students, will now be described in more details.

The 'Design and construct' project

The remit given to the students is that the company has been approached to produce a pre-production version of an electronic tachometer to be sold as a retrofit item to the car accessory market. The students' working tachometers are to match or better the price of the design used for an existing tachometer.

Students are given these details in the form of a handout that also indicates the aims of the assignment, the project organization, the assessment procedures, and a timetable (with milestones). In addition, they are also given supporting information on basic tachometer techniques. The milestones help ensure that if any group is not making adequate progress, then remedial action can be taken. Each of the milestones involves a short interview with a member of staff at which future progress is mapped out.

Group Selection

One aspect of particular importance is that of arranging for a suitable mix of group members. The groups are defined by the supervising staff based on their knowledge of the individuals. The criteria used are that groups must have a mixture of both first- and second-year students; must have both academically strong and weak members; must contain members known to be well-motivated and some whose motivation is questionable; students known to usually 'stick together' should be split up; and finally, as far as possible, groups should include a mix of students from different cultural backgrounds.

It is accepted that the above criteria will not lead to activities that run smoothly. However, the benefits that accrue warrant the extra support effort required.

Resources

To provide sufficient support for this time-constrained assignment a 'resource pack' is made available, containing data sheets on semiconductors, displays and commercial tachometers. It also gives indicators and references for further research.

A prototype tachometer has to be built. Groups are able to draw components from stores and order other components required. Technician support is available, both during and outside the formal workshop sessions, and is an invaluable and essential resource enabling the tight timetable to be adhered to.

A significant resource is of course, academic staff time. Groups are encouraged to treat staff as a resource and to use them to help with the design. This demands goodwill on the part of many members of the teaching staff, not just those who are directly involved in the assignment.

Assignment Operation, Assessment and Evaluation

The assignment falls naturally into three stages: initial project briefing and student group formation; design and production; and demonstration, report and group oral presentations.

Assessment is based on three elements: a critical individual review of the assignment by the student; staff assessment of the oral presentations; and staff assessment of the group report. For the last two items, peer assessment is used to distribute marks within each student group.

Each student is asked to complete an anonymous questionnaire to form the basis for evaluation. For the pilot course, the following general conclusions were drawn from the responses:

- the short timescale was not ideal;
- integration of practical work with the ghost company was well liked, although a minority of students were not convinced of the relevance;
- group skills were considerably improved;
- technical knowledge of electronics was improved;
- individual strengths and weaknesses of students were highlighted;
- the effectiveness of the assignment was improved by linking the assignment between course cohorts;
- leadership of each group was not necessarily given by second-year students; first-year leaders or no leader sometimes emerged;
- the use of peer assessment was useful in motivating weak or non-attending students.

Further development work

Whilst the feedback obtained shows that the assignment has worked well, it is clear that it can be improved. The need for more time is obvious. A more difficult problem is that of how to motivate those students who have a jaundiced view of the ghost company and the role of the assignment within it.

A proposal being examined is to try and increase the reality of the situation by the use of more convincing role play. For example, various members of the academic staff who already hold positions within the structure of the ghost company will be encouraged to take part in the progress interviews at the milestones.

A more detailed role allocation within each group is also likely. For example, the second-year students could be allocated the roles of project manager and senior project engineer, the first-year students being junior engineers.

Conclusions

Linking the assignment between consecutive years of the course has worked well and been found to improve the effectiveness of the project. Relating the assignment to the ghost company adds realism and motivation.

A sensitive balance is required in timescales so that students have sufficient time to complete the assignment, but on the other hand have tight deadlines and subsequent pressure to aid motivation. Peer assessment is a critical aid in persuading weak and non-attending students to contribute to the assignment.

Overall, this linked assignment has proved to substantially help in the development of the students' professional, personal and technical skills.

References

Bramhall, M D, Eaton, D E, Lawson, J S and Robinson, I M (1991) 'An integrated engineering degree programme: student-centred learning', in Smith, R (ed.) *Innovative Teaching in Engineering,* Chichester: Ellis Horwood.

Payne, R N, Robinson, I M, Short, C, Eaton, D E and Tidmarsh, D H (1992) 'A portfolio assessment scheme in engineering courses', in *Innovative Assessment in Higher Education,* University of Wales at Bangor.

Chapter Twenty

Management Indecision: Using Group-work in Teaching Creativity

Peter McHardy and Steven Henderson

Introduction

In this chapter we outline some thoughts on using group-based learning to incorporate creativity and intuitive learning into the curriculum. Many of the key ideas presented came from a brainstorming and reflection session undertaken by the business policy group at Leicester Business School.

Common pedagogical processes are designed to assist, or compel, students to acquire both a knowledge base and skills ownership. If during the process creativity, intuition and originality emerge, they are often regarded as extra qualities possessed by some learners and teachers and deserving special recognition. However, learning situations designed to encourage and develop such qualities are surprisingly rare, even though demonstration of originality of thought is commonly regarded as prerequisite to the award of the highest classes of honours degree.

The prevailing approach would be justified if the ability to be creative were regarded solely as a genetic gift, akin to ESP, or even magical.

However, if creativity is regarded as the novel application of ideas, knowledge and skill to a problem or situation, it would seem wrong to designate it as exceptional, so that it is not regarded as a legitimate extension or even culmination of the current skills and knowledge focus.

The knowledge/skills matrix

Figure 20.1, at the end of this chapter, was put together during the reflection session mentioned above and is presented here with some reservations. It attempts to model learning outcomes in terms of knowledge and skills acquired, with respect to common teaching methods.

We suggest here that learning takes the form of concave contour lines, originating from the north-west quadrant of the diagram. A business student first acquires some basic knowledge, from which elementary skills and techniques are drawn. These early achievements are then developed during a course, so that the learner has a toolkit of skills and knowledge to apply to identifiable situations. The more successful students will grasp opportunities to apply their skills to unfamiliar situations, and identify gaps in their knowledge which constrain activity in some way.

However, not all students will see these opportunities. In such cases, which we suggest include the majority of students, effectiveness is not so much limited by what is not known or skills which are insufficiently honed, but by some other gap, which we call the 'intuition gap', where existing skills and knowledge are insufficiently blended. Clearly, such blending occurs when business students become business practitioners and learn by their (often expensive) experience. However, we would argue that higher education can make a contribution to closing this 'intuition gap' by a more explicit encouragement of creative learning for all, rather than only the exceptional students. To put it another way, we would hold that businessmen and businesswomen need to be able to operate comfortably in the south-east quadrant of the diagram, given the increasingly uncertain, dynamic and chaotic business environment. However, most of their educational experiences will have been delivered using techniques best suited to other quadrants.

Most of the learning techniques identified in the south-east quadrant are group-based activities, and can be substantially different experiences from those we have assigned to other quadrants. In particular, the buzz, excitement and indiscipline observed in, say, a game of intuition is not normally encouraged in the classroom (or in many company board rooms – or indeed academic boards of study) where behaviour is often formalized, or even ritualized, to the point where there is little contribution to learning at all.

The experiences gained by students in such activities as a 'fish bowl' or a debate are often the most rewarding part of the learning process, especially where candidates review how they have progressed by analysing how they achieved complex decisions. Real-life pressures of time management, multiple decision making at group and individual level, and the ability to delegate issues and responsibilities, can be incorporated into scenarios which require some kind of analysis and, most importantly, decision making on the part of the group. For this kind of decision process-based activity, it is important that choices and options are not constrained – as in many business games – by the need to make decisions from a computer menu, or some other limitation imposed by an algorithm which models decision outcomes. In this respect, a business game in the south-east quadrant is significantly different to other kinds of business game.

Clearly, it is necessary to build learners up to this quadrant gradually, through progressively more difficult scenarios as their confidence in applying accepted knowledge and skills grows. This can be achieved through role-playing case studies and syndicate business game challenges involving, for instance, their own research into foreign cultures, and other unfamiliar settings, in which they are required to both analyse and make decisions.

Interestingly, the intuitive elements of any decision made can be unrecognizable in such outputs as presentations and formal reports. A natural first stage of decision making may well be instinctive, or based on intuition, but students will generally attempt to authenticate their decision with accepted theory and practice, so that what started as an intuitive feeling is given credibility by 'strategizing' it. Where such decision process activity is to be assessed, either for feedback or for a formal assessment grade, it is necessary for the activity to be videoed for subsequent analysis.

The implication of our learning model is that the kind of training offered in higher education may assist students to apply their knowledge and skills to making decisions which resolve well-defined problems, and to appreciate the factors which are significantly outside the range of such problems. But assisting students to apply the same skills and knowledge in a more flexible, creative and adventurous way will require different techniques. The remainder of this chapter is devoted to a description of one business game designed to complement traditional techniques in this way.

Management Indecision: the game

The business game described below is our attempt to push students into the creative (south-east) areas of the matrix described above. As such, it requires the students to apply standard business techniques to problems which they generate for themselves as the game progresses. There is no attempt to model the outcomes of these decisions in the manner of, say, a computer simulation game. We take the view that, providing the rationale for the decision is sound, the more important areas of creativity, decision taking and group-work should be developed in a non-deterministic fashion. The game was originally developed for a course at De Montfort University, but has also been used on our franchised HNC, where small modifications enabled it to be used as the prime vehicle for competence testing.

Each tutorial group must demonstrate application of basic marketing, personnel, managerial and accounting techniques to situations which develop as they introduce change into the company. Students are expected to work under sustained and increasing pressure of deadlines and organizational constraints. The accent is on the decision making, forcing students to experience both the process of and solutions to business problems.

Students begin by organizing themselves on company lines, electing their managing director and other senior staff from within their tutor group, (although they are required to demonstrate a competent understanding of the recruitment process) with areas of responsibility given to individual managers and departments. Each group has responsibility for choosing the products and markets in which the firm operates, but the business must be a manufacturing company and its span of operations must be broadly consistent with the inherited balance sheet. Successful groups have selected, for example, paper cartons, industrial toasters and garden gnomes.

Information (knowledge) inputs of strategic marketing, finance and manufacturing are given through formal lectures and appropriate videos. Practice and skills development are achieved through workshop tutorials, some of which are voluntary, others compulsory. Each group also has access to a tutor acting as facilitator through 'open' tutorials. Students are expected to use this input to find ways of achieving their mission by devising a strategic marketing plan, and introducing just-in-time manufacturing methods and total quality management to their factory. These plans can be constructed using such software as PLANVIEW.

The game works best at a fast pace, so that students are encouraged to think on their feet, analysing the theory after experiencing decision making under gradually accelerating pressure. Students will be exposed to crisis management techniques, short report writing and people management issues, putting into practice theory already learnt on their course. To give immediate relevance to the programme, each group visits a local manufacturing firm to get hands-on experience of production, engineering and capital investment issues, and their inherent advantages and problems. The game works best if lecturers play a facilitating role, treating the students as though they were already managers and implementors – after all, many entrepreneurs have already started to be business people while in the typical student age-band. Creativity, innovation and communication of missions and objective have a heavy weighting in the assessment.

The approach used enables us to incorporate such intuitive/creative and interactive learning techniques as role play and simulation into the learning and assessment strategy. Consequently, learning can be based on experience backed up by the lecture and tutorial programme. In order to facilitate the approach, learning activities are structured around a particular theme, such as flexible manufacturing, strategic marketing planning and so on. At the end of each theme, students make a short presentation to the rest of their tutorial group regarding aspects of the theme with particular relevance to the project.

There are no formal teaching inputs at the end of the game. Students are expected to finalize their plans, and a series of meetings are videoed. In these meetings, a strategic decision at board level is transformed into operational plans at departmental level – including negotiation with the work-force in the production department. A final meeting is necessitated by an unexpected emergency which requires immediate attention.

The programme requires students to manage themselves and their peers effectively, and to identify situations where their competence is insufficient to complete tasks to the required standard. Once these are identified by the students, remedial inputs are provided by staff, or the students are directed to other sources. By designing the programme in this way, it is intended that many principles of capability must be demonstrated by a successful student. In particular, planning and organizing the time and activities of themselves and their peers is imperative, as is efficient negotiation and delegation of areas of study and work within each tutorial group.

Assessment

The assessment strategy reflects our wish to assess students' ability to make business decisions and estimate likely consequences of their actions. Although the business concepts introduced to facilitate this, that is management accounting ratios, financial performance indicators and so on, are tested in their own right, we are principally interested in application and performance.

A prime aim of assessment is to focus the group's mind on the decision-making processes rather than on the plan itself. The assessment programme has three elements:

- As each group finalizes its plans, a series of meetings are videoed, as is the final meeting necessitated by the unexpected emergency. Credit is given to students able to show ability to manage organizational change in a controlled fashion, demonstrate an originality in their marketing ideas and respond quickly and intelligently to this unexpected crisis in the company. Capability is assessed by tutor examination of the videos: tutors look for evidence that students have managed themselves and their peers effectively.

- Five or six items of individual and group-work related to the development of their company. These include a presentation following an industrial visit; recruitment of a sales director; planning and designing an advertising campaign; controlling working capital; budgeting and forecasting; and strategic gap. In all cases, credit is given for intelligent application of an appropriate technique, and minor errors of theory and financial inaccuracy are tolerated.

- A short formal written examination – based on a seen case study – in which individuals propose solutions to specific business problems. The problems in the case study will be similar to those experienced by a student participating in the game itself.

All exercises and presentations count towards the students' final assessment grade for the module. Groups need to demonstrate that divisions of tasks and problems have been negotiated and delegated realistically, and that formal and remedial inputs provided by staff, industrial visits and educational videos have been taken on board.

Difficulties Encountered

There are two major sources of difficulty with the game. First, allowing the students to develop their own ideas and means of operation places great stress on commitment and a mature attitude. Where this game runs on courses in which tutors emphasize and develop these qualities anyway, initial confusion over what the students are actually required to do is remarkably short and painless. On the other hand, simply grafting this game onto traditional lecture and seminar programmes can cause genuine distress to both the students and staff.

The second area of difficulty is the 'open' nature of the game, which can cause serious bunching of staff contact hours and room allocations, particularly for students to hold their meetings in. These are compounded by the number of assessed activities run during the game. Often complicated one-off timetabling solutions are required. As timetables become more condensed and overcrowded, this constraint becomes more serious. Regrettably, it is the case that the game can no longer be fitted into some course schedules.

Summary

The purpose of the game is to simulate as near as possible what an actual business environment feels like. Student groups are given a set of accounts with which they invent their own manufactured product range. They then plan and implement a modernization strategy for their chosen business over a three-year time period, during which a threefold increase in turnover is expected. This is called 'Mission impossible', and runs throughout a whole module, culminating in each group being assessed on video whilst running their company in three vital areas of strategic decision making, implementation of manufacturing, and marketing plans. All students must appear on and contribute to the video.

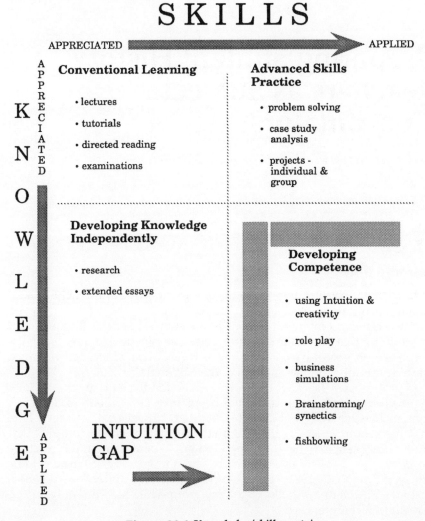

Figure 20.1 *Knowledge/skills matrix*

Chapter Twenty-one

Preparing Student History Teachers as Subject Coordinators

Sneh Shah

Introduction

Two virtually parallel developments are taking place in the field of education, each having been initiated independent of the other. However, the two can be combined to result in an improvement in the quality of the training that subject teachers receive. The two developments are the emphasis on group-based learning in the context of learner-managed learning, and the implementation of the National Curriculum.

In group-based learning the focus has tended to be on the methodology of group-work, such as the nature of peer assessment, and subject content has generally not been highlighted. However, it is argued here that the requirements of the National Curriculum are so complex that student teachers may be ill-equipped to implement them in the teaching environment if the traditional lecture/seminar approach continues to be adopted (see NCC, 1991). The example of training students as potential history coordinators will illustrate how group-work may not only be better, but in fact imperative.

Background to the new requirements

The new requirements raise three relevant issues. First the focus on subject specialism. It has long been pointed out that there is a close relationship between the knowledge of the subject which the teacher possesses and the quality of his or her training (see Alexander, *et al.*, 1992). The idea of the curriculum coordinator was developed to try to ensure that schools could make maximum use of the collective subject strength of staff. Specialist teachers can work in four different roles: that of the generalist, generalist/consultant, semi-specialist and specialist. The burden on teacher trainers becomes clear from the fact that every school will need to work out its own particular combination of teaching roles in the light of two principles: pupils' needs and staff strengths and flexibility.

Second, there is the issue of training teachers for the requirements of the National Curriculum (NCC, 1991). Her Majesty's Inspectorate, for example, found that main-subject history students need a well-structured taught component on curriculum leadership in schools. It seems that the training institutions have tended to train students to be history teachers rather than coordinators.

Third, the relationship between subject application and curriculum courses is especially important when financial constraints result in it not being possible for all the tutors, representing the different subjects and curriculum planning, to be present while the students are undergoing exercises.

Expectations for newly qualified primary teachers

Many of the expectations such as the ability to prepare, implement and evaluate lesson plans, assess children, and cater for all ranges of ability have been key features of the traditional history professional courses. There are now several additional new requirements. For example, the National Curriculum is making wider demands with regard to subject knowledge; teachers need the ability to link history teaching to that of other subjects; and pupils must be taught in multicultural and gender-equal cross-curricular themes. Finally, students need to have experience of leadership roles, develop communication and interpersonal skills including the capacity to work with others and be flexible according to the needs of the school.

The role of group-work

There are a number of reasons why group-work can be more effective as a means of preparing the student teachers to become subject coordinators than the use of traditional ways of teaching. These include the following:

- the new demands for history specialist students are more complex and demanding of knowledge and strategies than ever before;
- larger group sizes means that factors are added such as students following different age-phase specialisms, with their needs having to be met with less contact time available;
- the skills required for leadership are more effectively learnt in situations where students take responsibility for planning and discussing work with their peers;
- using groups means that more of the content can be covered in less time than in lectures, provided the structure is well thought out;
- having a mixture of students taking different age-phases, or taking different subject specialisms, is a real reflection of what could happen in a primary staff meeting;
- there are increased opportunities for students to relate their training to themselves individually;
- there is a chance to utilize the creative potential of every student, so that students' learning and input is not simply related to assessment.

Three stages of group-work

The approach described here has been tried at the University of Hertfordshire during the students' final year of training. A certain amount of subject information can therefore be assumed, as well as previous practical experience in schools.

There are three stages, the first two dealing with history subject specialists on their own and the third with specialists for not only history but also the whole range of primary school subjects.

Stage 1

First the whole group is presented with information to outline their topic, highlighting the particular dimension, with justification for the particular way in which the given National Curriculum dimension/theme has been interpreted, how the topic content and teaching methods have been designed for the dimension, and what selection choices have been made in relation to factors such as time available.

The students are divided into groups of not more than four on the basis of their age-phase specialism, for example, nursery, infant or junior. Each group is given a different study unit to focus on. This is designed to increase students' familiarity with the new study units, and with the type of content not traditionally taught to primary school children. A particular dimension is given to each group from the National Curriculum requirements, for example, gender aspects.

At the end of this stage the students will have some knowledge about a whole range of study units and their content; examples of ways in which the different dimensions/themes can be applied to study units; and further awareness of requirements of teachers dealing with age-phases other than their own.

Stage 2

The next stage takes the students into long-term planning for the school across all the age-phases. The National Curriculum requirements are complex, especially in that with prescribed aspects there are choices in the use of optional units and the order in which they are taken. Long-term planning ensuring continuity and progression for the children means that certain aspects have to be taken into account. For example, possible overlap of content with the core and supplementary units; the progression of children's learning as evidenced in the attainment target requirements; and the use of the different strategies in history teaching that maintain children's learning as well as interest.

The division of groups at this stage has to be based on the most appropriate way to get the students to experience the complexities and the alternatives to planning. The groups are then given one of a range of specific tasks.

Stage 3

By the completion of stage 2, the students will have become familiar in a practical way with the complexities of the National Curriculum requirements specifically for history, and will have gained confidence in making choices, and the rationale for them.

One aspect criticised in HMI reports is the division between subject tutors and curriculum planning tutors. It may be the case that subject tutors are not *au fait* with the issues and processes of curriculum planning. It is also possible that they may not be as familiar with the application requirements of other school subjects as would be necessary in order to implement the National Curriculum. The linking is expected to take place by way of the students.

In this way students are faced with the range of expertise that is likely to be found in a primary school, that is teachers specializing in specific subjects, while teaching all the primary school subjects. An appropriate way to complete this stage is for students to complete leadership checklists about themselves and about one other member of the group. These are then compared so that each individual student becomes even more aware of what may be required in a real school situation.

The role of the tutor

At this stage it does not appear that the groups can function without a tutor. This perhaps reflects the anxiety caused amongst students as well as primary school staff about being able to implement the history requirements. There is considerable interaction between the students and the tutor, and the way certain groups tackle the tasks will vary according to the group composition. However, because of the rigid requirements of the National Curriculum the agenda cannot be totally set by the students. Three specific roles can be identified for the tutor:

- to have updated information about history requirements and practices as the students are likely to feel worried about the tasks;
- to watch the working of groups carefully to keep them on task, prevent domination by any particular member and provide the correct impetus as necessary;
- to have enough information about the students themselves, and their teaching practice experiences to be able to draw these in as relevant.

The tasks for the tutors may appear to be easy but last year's experience has demonstrated that there has to be more preparation by the tutor. In addition, the methods needed to train subject specialists go well beyond the knowledge of history.

References

Alexander, R, Rose, J and Woodhead, C (1992) 'Curriculum organization and classroom practice in primary schools: A discussion paper', London: Department of Education and Science.

National Curriculum Council (1991) *Implementing National Curriculum History*, York: NCC.

Section Five:

Purpose-designed Modules Using Group-work

The benefits stemming from purpose-designing a module to include group-work are likely to far outweigh those gained from subsequently grafting it on, however skilfully. This section contains examples in which either group-work is the *raison d'être* of the course, or the course's whole philosophy and rationale make it the inevitable medium. Such purpose-designed modules are fortunately increasing in popularity, as others recognize the benefits and motivation that such courses engender.

Wilkinson at the University of Glasgow describes the way in which recognition of the needs of electrical engineering students for mathematics determines the approach to the subject. Group-work is the method which allows the course to achieve its aims, rather than being introduced for its own sake.

For rather different reasons, Nicholls from the Manchester Metropolitan University came to a group-based module for history students. Groups of students produce a resource pack for schoolchildren on the industrial revolution. The aims of the module here are the development of 'enterprise-related' skills, which are seen as being integral to successful group-related activities and at the same time operate as preparation for further 'independent study'.

Hassall and Lewis at Sheffield Hallam University put the purpose of the module itself squarely on the introduction of group-based learning *per se*. This skills-based approach is very appropriate for an accounting course, yet the specific objectives of the module are still fairly equally divided between personal skills and qualities and academic skills.

The last chapter in this section, by Hunt and McGovern at the University of Derby, aims to lead student teachers towards an understanding of how to operate as 'reflective practitioners'. As one of only two organizing concepts for the whole degree programme, the 'reflective practitioner' module uses a group-based learning environment seen as integral to the course rationale.

Chapter Twenty-two

Using Group-projects in the Teaching of Mathematics to Electrical Engineering Students

Judy Wilkinson

Introduction

Before designing a course to teach mathematics to engineers we should first consider the reasons why engineers need to learn mathematics. Engineers need to solve mathematical models of practical situations; for electrical engineers, these include electronic circuits, semiconductors, electrical machines and electrical systems. However, we are not trying to produce mathematicians or writers of software packages – we want to produce engineers who appreciate the scope and limitations of mathematical models of practical devices and who can choose and use the appropriate software to solve their models.

Engineers need to acquire the mathematical literacy to understand the mathematics used in books and papers on their subject. For instance, control engineers must know about Laplace transforms, where they come from and why they are used, but need not be able to work out a particular transform as long as they know where to find it and can follow a proof. Engineers also need a modicum of algebra to do 'back of the envelope' calculations, naturally and easily. Finally they must have the ability to choose the relevant software and check that a program is working correctly. It is fundamental to teaching mathematics using modern techniques that engineers can be confident about the results from a software package and know that a program is correct when they cannot check it by hand.

In the past mathematics was an individual enterprise: if you wanted to solve a new problem you had to understand and be able to carry out all the necessary steps yourself. With the advent of computers all engineers have access to routines and procedures written by mathematicians and software specialists. This implies that the work of mathematicians should be appreciated but not duplicated.

The two main areas to consider in teaching mathematics to engineers, therefore, are simple calculations and the use of software packages. To use a cooking analogy, students must learn to chop vegetables and cook them as well as select ingredients and make a balanced menu. They do not need to be experts in culinary chemistry.

Using group-work

Individuals need to develop their own skills to deal with simple algebraic formula. However, working in groups encourages them to discuss any conceptual difficulties with each other. Seeing another student work through a problem often helps to clarify their approach or suggests other methods of attack. Group-work can aid the understanding of mathematics and help the development of the student from a passive acceptor of information to a confident user of mathematical techniques.

We use software packages to enable students to carry out open-ended investigations and find that if they work in groups they help each other solve any problems with the software. This interaction also generates excitement and motivation. We want to develop the intellectual ability of the students so that they explore problems and integrate the mathematical results with the practical applications for themselves. This involves a careful selection of material, critical analysis of the learning outcomes and an environment which encourages the students to explore and discuss together.

Organization of the Course

At the University of Glasgow the class of between 60 to 80 electrical engineering students is divided into groups of four or five. The students are allowed to choose their groups with any newcomers assigned to existing groupings. The course is divided into two-week blocks with lecture notes given out, one lecture a week being used to explain and illuminate the notes. There is one tutorial based on calculations and manipulations and one investigation to be carried out, either on a programmable calculator or on the MathCad software.

Each group of students has to submit the tutorial solution and the investigation report each fortnight. These are marked and count for 40 per cent of the final mark for the course, individual students receiving the mark assigned to their group. In their first year the students have had tutorials in groups but have not been actively encouraged to collaborate, so the requirement that they submit one piece of work from the group on which they will be assessed is a new departure.

A selection of students are called to present their solutions; these presentations take between 15 and 20 minutes and are designed to check that no students are being 'carried' and that they understand the work that has been submitted in their name. If they cannot demonstrate their competence the mark is reduced. This is a harsh sanction but has the compensation that individual students are talked to, and staff can pick up problems and difficulties. If a group is not happy with one of the members it becomes apparent. This system also allows for the encouragement of weaker students through exploration of some of the problems with them. All students have an oral at some time in the year, but those students with problems may be seen more regularly.

The course has two hours a week allocated for lectures, one of these being replaced by the group-work. Lecture notes and directed reading lists are distributed and an attempt is made to highlight the main concepts during the lecture hour rather than writing notes on the board. In the hour set aside for students to work on the tutorials or investigations they may arrange to meet elsewhere or at another time. Originally it was thought that students might have difficulty in finding space or time to work together but this does not seem to be a problem.

Up to half the groups may run into difficulties and want guidance. Students do actually discuss the work, and sessions are more fruitful than usual tutorial sessions in which students work individually and often ask trivial questions because they have not discussed the work before attending. However, individuals – usually those who have conceptual difficulties which have not been answered by peer discussion – also approach staff directly.

Problems in Organization

Students are asked to form themselves into groups of four or five. For the majority of students this works very well. They see their friends regularly and can organize to work together. The problems arise with the few people who are either repeating, are direct entries or have no friends. For example, a student may cause concern because he does not turn up regularly and has not contributed to the group, so he is getting into the position where he will fail the course because he has not submitted the work. In this case he is seen individually, written to and counselling is suggested. Some other students resent continuous assessment, preferring to work at the last minute for examinations and make little effort through the rest of the year. These students are told that continuous assessment is a requirement that they should pay attention to. Industrial life resembles continuous assessment rather than occasional examinations.

The combination of giving out lecture notes and directed reading is not used in any other course in the department so the students are not familiar with this approach. It is causing the most difficulty where some students have not read the notes and expect staff to act as authority in the usual way, whereas others are questioning and probing quite deeply. It is difficult and tiring to handle a true open discussion situation with a large class, especially if trying to tease out the problem behind some of the questions or find examples that illuminate the student's point rather than give a straightforward exposition. Discussions occur spontaneously since students come prepared and having read the material. Some students are interested and want to join in, but others resent this 'waste of time'. There is a potential danger that students still expect questions to be answered immediately without time for reflection.

Staff and Student Reaction

Staff reaction is mixed. Some view it as an exciting way to teach and agree that it motivates most of the students. However, mathematics is a subject that arouses great passion and some staff believe it is an individual activity and that students cannot gain from group-work. These people are also very suspicious of students using mathematical software, believing that you must gain a very high standard of competence before you can use a computer package.

Many students work together anyway, so are happy to do so when solving problems. The sheets ask them all to sign the work to confirm that they have seen it and agreed with it. The person who writes it up has to make this clear and sign it. Presentation of mathematics is important and in most groups the students come to the discussion bringing their own solutions and argue for a joint effort. The proportion of the final mark given to group activities is sufficient to persuade them take the work seriously.

Tutorials and Investigations

The tutorial and investigation material has been chosen to encourage students to explore contexts and enjoy creativity in an environment where they are supported by their peer group. Many students enjoy mathematics because they know that they get an answer that is correct and there is no discussion or argument. As any move towards more independent learning is met with occasional hostility, the investigations were carefully structured.

They are introduced to MathCad by getting them to type in a program, but then have to analyse the results and relate them to a physical problem. The manual and staff are available but there is no permanent assistant present so students have to help each other sort out problems with the software. This is very successful. From the results of a questionnaire it seems that 80 per cent feel fairly confident that they can use the software to solve problems other than those detailed in the investigation sheet.

Another exercise encourages them to explore the limits of accuracy of their calculators and explain certain results. Some of them are not happy about the 'guesstimates' and value judgements required in this. The work leads to a lot of discussion and argument. Finally, work on interpolation encourages students to analyse some of their laboratory experiments, giving them a free choice in the material they select and the software program they use.

Because these are second-year students on a four year honours degree course in the Scottish university system, they still need some reassurance and to have work which is uncontroversial with clear objectives. This is provided by the tutorials which involve straightforward calculations and manipulations. There has been some worry here that students will allow one member of their group to write up the solutions.

However, the orals supply an element of control that, in most cases, encourages them to consult. It seems that because the work counts and the students are giving in a joint effort most of the tutorials are well written out and the investigations are well documented. It takes an average of between five and ten minutes to mark each piece of work. The orals take about 15 minutes per student with a small number seen two or three times.

Concluding remarks

Group-working in mathematics encourages the students to discuss the concepts and learn for themselves. If it is carefully structured, monitored and assessed with the tutorials and reports counting for a significant part of the final mark, it provides an environment in which they learn to value the views of their peers and contribute to the group. Time then becomes available during which a member of staff can address individual difficulties and act as a facilitator rather than as the authority, with students acting as passive receptors.

Chapter Twenty-three

History Resource Packs for Schools

David Nicholls

Background

As part of a project, six history students at the Manchester Metropolitan University have produced a resource pack for a local school. The pack is called 'The industrial revolution: A study of the social and working conditions of factory workers in Victorian England', and is designed for use by schoolchildren of around 13 years of age. This chapter explains the genesis and operation of the project and seeks to draw some lessons from the experience of running it.

The group-project was devised in order to offer a unit to second-year undergraduates that would prepare them for an established third-year option called 'Independent study in history'. The latter is a placement course which involves students in project work on behalf of external clients, and which foregrounds enterprise-related skills (Nicholls, 1992). The new course unit was intended to allow students the opportunity to cultivate the particular skills that are integral to successful group-related activities – interpersonal and collaborative, negotiating and communicative, and evaluative and decision-making skills, along with other valuable competences, such as time management, computing, and presentational abilities. In this way, the schools project was perceived as a useful adjunct to 'Independent study', supplementing and complementing the student's range of personal and transferable skills.

It was decided to offer it as an option within an established and compulsory second-level course entitled 'Approaches to the study and methods of history', which is taught for three hours per week for the whole of the academic year. This is divided into three parts: a general introduction in which students explore the development of history as a discipline, followed by two consecutive ten-week optional units which foreground historiographical, methodological, and theoretical issues. 'Approaches' is an appropriate site for the schools project in that the latter requires students to handle historical sources, to display skills relevant to historical training, and to engage with methodological issues including the contemporary concern about the relationship between an historical education and the world of work as posed by the Enterprise Initiative.

The schools project

Several local schools were approached as potential clients, and an arrangement reached with Wilmslow High, with a history teacher who was both willing and pleased to participate in the project. The teacher was supplied with written and verbal information about the course unit. It was agreed that the group would negotiate a suitable project directly with her and that the level at which it would be pitched and any special requirements would be made clear to the students at the outset. The possibility of ongoing projects to be taken up by students in future years was also floated at this stage.

Six students elected to take the new unit. This proved to be an ideal number both in terms of group dynamics and for the production of a viable resource pack. Prior to the commencement date, the students visited Wilmslow High and agreed with the teacher concerned the topic on which they would be working. They had an open brief to settle on any subject that was deemed appropriate, useful and viable. The teacher directed the students towards the industrial revolution because it dovetailed neatly with one of her classes, and the students happily fell in with this choice because of the ready availability of source materials.

The course unit guide informed students that they would be 'expected to work on their own, and collaboratively; to negotiate with, and meet the requirements of, the school-teachers; and to produce a pack which demonstrates a mastery of computer skills'. There would be no formal weekly class contact. A preliminary meeting would be held to get the project underway, followed by two further meetings, the first to report progress midway through the course, the second to discuss the completed pack and provide feedback. The students, however, were encouraged to call by at any time if there was any aspect of the project that they wished to discuss.

In terms of the organizational mechanics of the course, most stress was placed upon the importance of group activities. The educational experience of the students had hitherto emphasized individual attainment and competition rather than collaboration and mutual support in the process of learning. The students now had to organize their own meetings, agree on a division of labour, liaise with the teacher, and coordinate the production of the resource pack. They did not find this easy. They quickly learned that progress could be interrupted or fouled up by the non-cooperation of any one member of the group – for example, by the failure to attend meetings or by tardiness in the production of scheduled contributions. Feedback from the more conscientious members of the group alerted me early on to some of these internal tensions – to displeasure with the recalcitrant individual who preferred to work on his own terms, and to distrust of the capabilities of the student charged with the task of producing the pack in desktop publishing form.

The students had agreed a division of labour at their first meeting. Five of them would each work on a particular theme: working conditions and leisure; living conditions; health and welfare; working-class education; and factory reform. The sixth would coordinate the progress of the pack, advise the group on areas of overlap, write an introduction to it, and learn the necessary skills to produce it in desktop form. Each section was to be word-processed using a package that could be downloaded on to an Apple Macintosh for the final production. The assessment arrangements were adjusted for the sixth member of the group so as to place greater weight on his organizational and presentational skills.

Assessment and Evaluation

The procedures for assessing the unit had been partly determined by the regulations of the course unit as a whole. Under those regulations, students were normally expected to complete a 1,500-word essay for each of the two options and to answer three questions in a three-hour examination, one from each part of the course (that is, the general introduction and the two optional elements). These arrangements were modified for students taking the group project. Their individual contributions to the resource pack took the place of an examination question and were assessed on the basis of a range of criteria which included, *inter alia*, content, appropriateness for the intended audience, and presentation. The students sat a two-hour paper on the other parts of the 'Approaches' course. The standard essay was replaced by a report on the group-project as a whole, in which the students were asked to provide three things:

- a critical account of the setting up, negotiation, and putting together of the resource pack. The purpose of this was to introduce an element of reflection into the learning process, which can be at least as important as the reality of the experience itself;

- a piece of self-assessment, that is a critical reflection on the student's own contribution to the planning and production of the group-project;
- peer assessment, that is a critical assessment of the other members of the group in terms of their role in the project and the quality of their assignments.

The unit as a whole was monitored and evaluated in two ways: by the students themselves and by the teacher. At the final tutorial meeting, the students gave verbal feedback which supplemented their written reports. The consensus was that the experience had been a valuable one. They were immensely pleased with the final product, and derived particular satisfaction from the knowledge that it would be used in the classroom and not put away and forgotten about as usually happened with the product of their labours. Indeed, they were keen to use the pack themselves with a class, and this was arranged with the teacher. Two of the group reported that the experience had stimulated their interest in pursuing teaching as a career.

The main problem the students had encountered was the novelty and difficulty of working as a group, but they acknowledged that the experience had taught them a good deal about organizational issues and interpersonal working relations. The feedback meeting took place in the presence of one of Her Majesty's Inspectorate who, coincidentally, was visiting the university to assess the humanities/social studies degree. He was suitably impressed with the resource pack, commented favourably upon the operation of the group-project, and expressed support for its educational objectives.

The schoolteacher at Wilmslow High kindly agreed to complete a questionnaire to provide additional valuable feedback. She was asked to place the individual contributions in order of merit, and this for the most part confirmed my own assessment of their relative qualities; to comment on the 'fitness for purpose' of the pack; and to make suggestions for future projects.

Lessons drawn

Some useful lessons can be drawn from this small experiment in group project work. First, there is no doubt that the most rewarding outcome for all its participants was the completion of a utilizable piece of educational equipment. The cover was produced by the Educational Services Unit of the university which also assisted with the final layout. Certain grammatical, stylistic, spelling and factual errors were corrected before the pack was printed for use by the school. Multiple copies were paid for by the

Enterprise Office. Otherwise, the work was entirely that of the students themselves, and they were justifiably proud of that achievement.

However, this pleasing outcome was not produced without friction within the group as described above. These tensions are part of the learning process and should not be discounted, but they do pose a very difficult question for teachers who want to introduce group-based methods into the curriculum. To what extent should they impose constraints upon the freedom of students to learn from their own experiences? One of the classic dilemmas of liberalism is here writ small: namely, how far should the freedom of the individual be allowed to interfere with the rights and liberties of the group at large? The capacity to hang oneself when given too much rope is always a serious matter but is especially so when the suicidal proclivities of the one can have a damaging effect upon the fortunes of the many, as in collaborative ventures.

The shift from structured forms of teaching to the participative learning process entailed by group-work brings with it many challenges for students and demands from them new types of competence, such as setting their own targets, negotiating between themselves and others, coping with the advantages and disadvantages of sharing tasks, understanding the dynamics of shared activities (leadership roles, cooperation, interpersonal relationships and so on). The tutor's dilemma comes from determining precisely how far to intervene to manage this activity in such a way as to maximize its advantages while protecting individual members of the group from the shortcomings of one or more of their colleagues.

Peer assessment played something of a regulating role here. It acted as a check upon individuals inclined to opt out of their obligations to the group, and allowed the more diligent to appraise the limitations of their peers. The students were remarkably frank about their respective merits, and broadly in agreement about a rank-order. Indeed, apart from a tendency to overvalue each other's work in terms of raw marks, their order of merit was very much in line with my own assessment.

However, experience of operating the course, coupled with student feedback, convinced me that peer assessment had to be backed up by other strategies to assist in and regulate the successful operation of group-based learning. The tendency had been to underestimate the uncertainties which the students had about collaboration, much of it coming from lack of experience. In future, therefore, they will receive careful counselling and advice at the first meeting. Moreover, it will be made a requirement of the course that they keep a diary of their involvement with the project. This will provide the basis for discussion at the mid-course meeting, for monitoring the progress of the group, the contribution of each individual within it and will form part of their assessment. Finally, students will be given more detailed guidance on peer assessment with the aim of showing them how to support subjective appraisals with objective criteria.

Concluding remarks

The production of resource packs and other project work for schools has great potential as a mechanism for introducing group-based learning methods into the higher education curriculum. The practice described here could be applied to disciplines other than history. Working with schools has advantages over links with other external clients in that the teachers have a ready grasp of the pedagogic issues involved. Moreover, teachers, lecturers and students have a natural empathy derived not just from a shared discipline but from an involvement in and commitment to education and learning.

Finally, once a unit of this sort is up and running, it has the potential to absorb large numbers of students in cost-effective programmes that are none the less intellectually stimulating, and thereby addresses one of the major issues confronting higher education in the 1990s. A tutor could manage several project-groups, as one alternative to the soulless grind of the large, formal class. The number of possible topics is virtually limitless. There is no shortage of local schools with which to work.

Before collaborative work can achieve greater purchase within the English education system, a paradigmatic shift in educational culture is required, a move away from the traditional emphasis on individual and competitive and towards more social and cooperative forms of learning. Such a change requires that students come to be more generally recognized and treated as active participants in their own learning, to the point where they become sufficiently confident of their own abilities to want to share them in peer-group activities. At the same time, they will come to see their fellow students as a resource upon which they can draw in their educational progress. Hopefully, such a significant change in educational culture and practice will be encouraged by the gradual and incremental introduction of group-based learning activities of the type described here.

Reference

Nicholls, D (1992) 'Making history students enterprising: independent study at Manchester Polytechnic', *Studies in Higher Education*, 17 , 1, 67–80.

Chapter Twenty-four

The Development and Implementation of Group-based Learning on an Accounting Degree

Trevor Hassall and Sarah Lewis

Introduction

The BA (Hons) in Accounting and Management Control at Sheffield Hallam University contains a final-year core subject, financial decision making, which in 1990 won the Partnership Award presented by Coopers and Lybrand for group skills in accountancy. The module was designed with the aim of introducing group-based learning.

The financial decision-making module

The specific objectives for this group-based learning programme were identified as follows:

- *Personal skills and qualities*

  Students should have identified and developed:
  - the ability to work within a group and the communication skills involved;
  - the negotiation skills necessary in identifying and analysing a problem and proposing solutions within a group;
  - the need within a group to allocate tasks and motivate others;
  - recognition and acceptance of leadership qualities and skills;
  - intra- or inter-group presentation skills; and
  - the ability to question assumptions, listen to arguments and respond accordingly.

- *Academic skills*

  Students should be able to:
  - identify the particular subject skills and knowledge appropriate to a particular problem;
  - appreciate the difficulties involved in clearly defining problem areas;
  - apply and integrate previously acquired subject skills and knowledge; and
  - evaluate, classify and organize information into a suitable format for the application of decision-making techniques.

The course is delivered through the medium of case studies. These are chosen so as to help examine problem situations of a broad business nature. Students work in different groups for each case. Role-play and structured tasks foster the integration of subject knowledge, personal skills and creative thinking processes. The aim here is to enable students to develop and apply an integrated approach to problem solving and to understand the problems inherent in the application of discipline-based knowledge to practical situations during a period of change.

The course then has two focal points: first the application and integration of discipline-based knowledge from a final-year programme and, second, the development of group skills. This means that learning in a group situation is occurring in two distinct but related areas. The students are expected to apply and integrate academic knowledge using the pedagogic device of case studies. The case studies are conducted in groups so the students are developing at the same time the personal skills associated with working in a group.

The process of development and implementation of the financial decision-making module raised many theoretical and practical issues. In reviewing the development and implementation of group-based learning in the module we have identified four areas; these are: justification issues, operational issues, assessment issues and evaluation issues. These are by no means mutually exclusive and in practice tend to interact with each other.

Justification Issues

The first problem when introducing the idea of group-based learning into the accounting degree was that the method was new. Or was it? Have students not been gathering in groups to discuss their studies for as long as students have been studying? Of course the latter type of group activity was informal. What we were attempting to introduce came within the formal framework of the course.

There was some resistance to the introduction of this element. Was this a general reaction to change or were there specific concerns in this instance? There are, it seems, two major but interrelated concerns emanating from the introduction of this method to a degree scheme. The first is quite simply to identify the exact educational process that is being attempted. This is perhaps best illustrated by considering how the potential outcomes might be expressed. Are you trying to educate or develop the individual in isolation, or are you trying to educate or develop the individual within a wider perspective, that is within a group? Traditionally the education model has seen learning as an individual activity, pursued and perhaps most importantly tested at the individual level.

The second concern is the connected issue of assessment; practical issues are dealt with as a separate item. However it is very difficult to separate this completely from the validation issue. Should the course assess the individual, or the individual as part of a group? There is without doubt unease in the area of assessment when it moves away from a straightforward assessment of a specific individual in an individual situation and moves to any extent towards either the assessment of an individual as part of a group, or the assessment of a group which is then related to the individual.

There are undoubtedly pressures for change in respect of the approach to group learning. The issues' incorporation into courses will be subject to validation of some kind. Clear answers need to be found to some of the above questions for the process to continue.

Operational Issues

Perhaps the greatest problem in operational terms is time allocation. We now recognize that case study activity should fall into three distinct phases. The first phase is case briefing, in which the case is presented and explained to the students. Students must be clear on two major items. First, what is expected of them in terms of output; this might be a group report, a group presentation to staff or the preparation by the group of a videoed presentation. The video is especially useful for later analysis and feedback on presentation skills. Second, students must be clear on the precise organization in terms of group membership and structure, if any is prescribed.

The second phase involves the preparation and presentation of the case as an activity. This is approached in one of two ways. On some occasions the students are asked to prepare informally as a group (with no members of staff present) and then make some form of formal presentation later to members of staff. On other occasions students are asked to do some general preparation on an informal basis and are then presented with the specific problem and required to solve it as a group while being observed by members of staff.

The final phase, in retrospect the most important, is the debriefing. This involves reviewing two distinct areas. The group's answer to a particular problem must be reviewed in academic terms, and their performance as a team must also be reviewed. This is for most academics undoubtedly the activity that causes most concern; it highlights an area in which the academics themselves need some further training. Our own experience suggests that students are very receptive to constructive comment on their performance and in many instances are not only aware of their own performance in a particular exercise but are very willing to be self-critical.

The other major operational area to highlight is group formation. Should groups be established which operate unchanged for a period of time or should groups be formed and reformed on a continual basis? We have established a practice in which no group should remain intact for more than a maximum of two case studies. This is based on the feeling that in practice people will usually be asked to work in groups that are forming and reforming on a regular basis.

Also, most people will have limited control in terms of the other members of the group they may be required to work with. This leads us to randomly generate group membership when the groups are changed. Perhaps the most positive comment we have had from students concerns this area. The students initially resent being made to work as a member of a group they have not been involved in the selection of, but after the event they appreciate considerably the skills they have developed in terms of group socialization.

Assessment Issues

This is one of the main problems in that the course requires assessment to be of individuals. The difficulty is how to arrive at an individual mark for a course that is conducted on a group basis. We do not claim to have found the answer, but can at least outline our present stage of development.

The course is assessed by 50 per cent examination and 50 per cent continuous assessment. The continuous assessment consists of two separate case studies; in the first the students are required to prepare a group presentation and are awarded a group mark. The second case study is in two parts, a group presentation with again a group mark and an individual report, each being given equal weighting. The examination consists of a pre-seen case study, the proposed solution to which is to be written up under time-constrained examination conditions. The examination is open-book and it is accepted that the students will do some preparation for it in groups.

In the past we experimented with forms of peer-group assessment. However, due to a greatly increased number of students taking this module and related time-constraints, it now proves impossible to continue with this activity.

Evaluation Issues

The course is subject to an overall evaluation in terms of the school of financial studies and law's internal quality assurance procedures. This is done by a course questionnaire that asks students to express their relative satisfaction/dissatisfaction with various aspects of each module. Comment has in the main been favourable but any deeper analysis does not readily flow from this source. During the next academic session one of the main developments the course team wish to implement is a questionnaire solely concerned with this unit. This should be designed to enable an analysis of students' perceptions of the changes in their group skills.

Concluding remarks

The module is designed to develop both academic and group skills. Learning about groups and learning within groups is one of the central objectives of the module. Perhaps the key issue is that this is relatively less structured and less formal than other courses of a more academic nature. The ability of staff and students to cope with this change in approach may well be the major factor in determining continued success.

Chapter Twenty-five

Towards the Reflective Practitioner

Pamela Hunt and Robert McGovern

Background

For students on BEd courses school experience is central to the course, informing students' understanding of the physical, social, moral and intellectual development of children and the management of their learning. Students are asked to undertake structured observations of children which focus attention on the effective management of group learning, methods of control, teaching styles and classroom organization.

The college-based course then seeks to negotiate students' understandings of these issues by organizing taught sessions in ways which allow shared understandings to be articulated and further developed. Thus the management of effective learning is both a professional and a personal concern of every student – the effective management of childrens' learning is considered alongside their own learning and students are exposed to the notion of their own empowerment through the creation, for themselves, of 'new' knowledge validated through experience and action research.

Course structure

The module described here is located in the second year of the BEd degree at the University of Derby. Its purpose is to produce entrants to the teaching profession who are capable and confident practitioners, committed to promoting the education of children in the primary age range and to their own continuing professional development. They are expected to achieve practical competency in delivering the National Curriculum based upon an informed understanding of the learning needs of young children and a critically informed awareness of the broader social and economic contexts in which children in this society learn and develop.

'Professional studies' is made up of *curriculum studies*, which aims to equip students with the subject and pedagogical knowledge necessary for them to plan and teach the subjects of the National Curriculum, and *educational studies*, the subject of this discussion. This module aims to synthesize school experience, or teaching practice, educational theory and reflection on practice. Central to educational studies is school-based and school-focused work. Observation of children and their teachers provides a challenging and meaningful way to examine theory and to develop a critical framework for the interpretation and evaluation of practice.

Throughout the four years of the BEd course two main organizing concepts inform the educational studies programmes of study: 'children growing and developing', and 'developing the reflective teacher'. In order that these organizing concepts can be effected, students are introduced to action research techniques and develop these throughout the programme. The intention is to allow students to conceive of themselves as 'reflective practitioners' engaged in 'research-based teaching', building firm foundations for future professional development and the generation of an effective professional knowledge to guide practice generally.

The students in question spend the second year specifically focusing on the education of children from 7 to 11 years of age. Consistent with the overall rationale, students examine the ways in which children develop and learn, and the role of the teacher in the later primary years. The pattern of the taught course is such that the 26 hours available are timetabled to prepare for, and to debrief, school experience.

Rationale for the course

So how were we to translate all this into a course consisting of only eight sessions spread throughout the year? In our planning meetings, we soon realized that we share a common view of learning and teaching. We could both recount instances when teachers on in-service training courses had made comments such as 'the children keep coming to me to check that they're doing the right thing' (teacher explaining how much she felt under pressure in the classroom). Or 'I haven't done anything because I wasn't sure what you wanted' (teacher explaining why a pre-course task had not been attempted).

These statements and countless others like them exemplify for us a view of teaching which has long predominated in our educational system and which, as Lawton (1989) has pointed out, has now received formidable support in the form of the National Curriculum. In this view, the very nature of knowledge, as well as the means of acquiring it, is mediated to the learner by some higher authority. The model is of a hierarchy and Chaplin (1988) argues that we use this most of the time in Western culture.

This 'teacher knows best' stance is highlighted by Glasser (1969) who warns that '... we err seriously if we take for granted that students can see the relevance in certain material just because we can.'

However, growing from the work of humanistic psychologists such as Maslow and Rogers, a view of learning has been gaining strength in which, as Ferguson (1982) describes:

... the learner is encouraged to be awake and autonomous, to question, to explore all corners and crevices of conscious experience, to seek meaning, to test outer limits, to check out frontiers and depths of the self.

The theory of phenomenology also lends support to the notion that in any learning situation each learner experiences a unique reality and that what is learned from this experience is therefore specific to the individual. Similarly, the theory of personal constructs (Kelly, 1955) adds to our understanding of the 'structure of the learner'. He argues that each of us organizes our already unique perceptions of others into a limited number of bipolar constructs. To realize our own narrow field of interpretation and to extrapolate from this that other people are operating from within quite different, but equally valid, restricted categories is a salutary experience. It makes nonsense of the notion that there is any objective truth which can be 'known' by teachers and transmitted to learners. Learners must instead help each other to learn for themselves. In other words, they must learn in groups.

Much has, of course, been written about the value of group-work for children. Slavin et al. (1985) sum up the results of several studies and suggest that the advantages of group-work include: productivity, creativity and efficiency (where tasks are concerned); and satisfaction, intrinsic motivation, positive self-concept, willingness to express ideas and feelings, willingness to become involved in learning activities, and prejudice reduction and liking of peers (as socio-emotional factors). The literature relating to the professional development of adults also supports the view that structured discussion in a cooperative group situation is valuable and the same advantages as those listed above are identified.

In addition, Garry and Cowan (1986) identify participative workshop sessions as providing the supportive environment in which adults can develop both their abilities and their confidence.

Implementation

This rationale, then, became the basis of our organization of the sessions, with the maximum amount of time given to learning in groups. At the start of the course, we use materials adapted from the Polytechnics and Colleges Funding Council's booklets, *Independent Learning with More Students* (Rust *et al.*, 1992) to make explicit some of the processes involved in effective group-work.

In the second session we introduce a 'jig-saw' activity. Students begin work in a 'home group'; then each 'home group' member is given a different paper on teaching styles on which to become an 'expert'. To do this, new groups are formed, consisting of those students who have the same paper to study. After a period for study and discussion, the 'experts' return to their 'home groups' where they each contribute what they have learned to a concluding discussion.

In the third session we supply students with a timed and resourced group workshop activity, designed to be facilitated by group leaders. For each session we also provide materials derived from *Curriculum in Action* (Ashton *et al.*, 1980), a pack for in-service teachers which enables them to evaluate what actually happens in their classrooms. We have called our materials 'Year 2 school tasks' and they are specific to this particular course in that they support the areas of study which are to be covered. They give general guidance concerning classroom observation, building on similar materials provided for the Year 1 education studies course, and then specify a sequence of activities. These involve the making of 'on-the-spot' classroom observation notes during days spent in school. The data collected then become the basis of collaborative analysis in the education studies sessions back at the university.

In using their analysis of their own observation notes as the starting point for discussion, the students are helped to understand the difference between the conceptualization of experience and the simple anecdotal description of it. Additionally, since work in pairs is usually suggested as a preliminary to larger group discussion we hope to support those students who, as Easen (1985) recognizes, are intimidated by anything which suggests 'public speaking'.

Concluding remarks

Whether or not we shall achieve our aim of fostering the development of 'reflective practitioners' by means of our course remains to be seen.

A pre-course questionnaire on attitudes to group-work indicated that the majority of students were favourably inclined towards this style of learning. For example, 75 per cent of them felt that discussing in a group helped them to sort out their own ideas while 80 per cent did not find it at all confusing to have to listen to the ideas of other group members.

A post-course evaluation is intended, to identify the success of group-learning strategies. Meanwhile, we certainly enjoy the sessions, and feedback from our students indicates that they are already making links between the course and their school experience, as hoped. Most exciting-ly, they tell us that they feel they are indeed taking charge of their own learning.

References

Ashton, P M E, Hunt, P, Jones, S and Watson, G (1980) *Curriculum in Action: Practical classroom evaluation*, Buckingham: Open University Press.

Chaplin, C (1988) *Feminist Counselling in Action*, London: Sage.

Easen, P (1985) *Making School-Centred INSET Work: A school of education for teachers*, Beckenham: Croom Helm/Open University.

Ferguson, M (1982) *The Aquarian Conspiracy*, London: Paladin.

Garry, A and Cowan, J (1986) *Learning from Experience: A tutor's guide to the use of small groups in continuing professional development*, Further Education Unit.

Glasser, W (1969) *Schools Without Failure*, London: Harper and Row.

Kelly, G A (1955) *The Psychology of Personal Constructs*, Vols I and II, New York: Norton.

Lawton, D (1989) *Education, Culture and the National Curriculum*, London: Hodder and Stoughton.

Rust, C et al. (1992) *Independent Learning with More Students*, Polytechnics and Colleges Funding Council.

Slavin, R et al. (1985) *Learning to Co-operate, Co-operating to Learn*, London: Plenum Press.

Part Three: Postscript

Chapter Twenty-six

Present Challenges
Roy Gregory and Lin Thorley

Where are we now?

The increasingly widespread use of group-work, as reflected by the chapters in this book, is adding significantly to the learning experience of our students. Our major challenge for the future is to address the many issues that group-work has raised. From the evidence here, practitioners in group-based learning are already actively working on many of these, but it seems appropriate to raise some of them here before moving on. In doing so we try particularly to pick up those issues that are implicit in the contributions to this book, but which are not necessarily discussed explicitly. Some of what we say here is personal opinion, but we make no apology for that: we must all establish our own viewpoint and we simply add ours to the debate, in the hope that it might be helpful to others rather than be prescriptive.

Any perspective on group-work should emphasize that it is not appropriate for all learning occasions with all students. Variety is important: we need to provide a learning environment which recognizes that different people have different ways of learning and that some will find group-learning uncongenial or difficult. Also, some tasks are by their nature unsuitable for group-learning. In course design it is important to look for a balance and range of delivery methods as well as for a balance and range of content.

Group-work is not without its problems. These can arise because its use as a method is inappropriate, at other times the cause is insufficient structure, unprepared students, poor course design or poor management by the tutor. Tutors themselves may have little experience of working in or managing groups and may thus be unaware of potential difficulties. In their own working lives in higher education lecturers are seldom expected to work in truly collaborative fashion; hence tutors may themselves not be actively practising the very skills they are asking their students to acquire. In such circumstances it is all too easy to be insensitive to the difficulties that can arise for students.

Working in groups can, unfortunately, have the effect of encouraging some individuals to opt out of the learning situation. This will then actually reduce the quality of the students' experience and may also demotivate others. The group-work has then, with all its potential for personal engagement with the subject matter, actually produced a passive approach to learning. Group-work can, too, be intimidating for some students and does not necessarily give them the personal freedom which may be offered by the anonymity of the lecture. Working individually, students can learn at their own pace, at times that suit them, with their own personal level of commitment.

Costing group-work

The current reduction in resources in higher education is in some cases encouraging an increase in group-work for the wrong reasons. We must make sure group-work is not used purely with the intention of saving staff time. Indeed, though group-work has well-known educational benefits when used appropriately, it does not always save staff time overall. Although staff may not need to be present during the learning event itself extra time is generally spent in the development and planning phase. There are often considerable start-up costs in group-work. It is important that we do not allow hidden time costs to reduce time available for students generally and thus reduce overall delivery quality.

Calculating the costs in terms of staff time should include time for writing the material, delivery, informal tutoring and monitoring of groups, assessment and evaluation. We must not just rely for costings on pilot studies run by enthusiasts. Enthusiasts will tend to make most things work and may underplay the real time spent.

There may be good reasons for expending extra resources – such as staff time – on particular areas, so that the investment will pay off later in the students' course. Working with students intensively in small groups early on in a course, for example, may be justified to encourage productive self-help groups which will be cost-effective later. It is important, though, that we are fully aware of the extent of the investment we are making.

Another helpful, but much less used, kind of 'costing' is of student learning hours. This can be useful in monitoring student work-loads. Staff can estimate the length of time that an average student, or group of students, might be expected to spend on an assignment. Without the conscious use of estimated learning hours staff tend with group-work to underestimate the necessary time taken and may unwittingly overload students.

What is learnt in groups?

Group learning faces higher education with challenges in what students learn, in the way they learn it and in the way they should be assessed. Much group learning is likely to be experiential. This must be taken into account in course design and delivery. It is helpful if it is made explicit to students in the exercise brief and assessment philosophy, so that students are aware of the direction they should be taking. It can also be useful to explain to students the essence of the experiential learning cycle, and its phases of doing, reviewing, theorizing and planning (Kolb, 1984). This helps students build a mental framework for their activities.

Sufficient time should be allowed for feedback to students. They will probably need to be encouraged in the reflection/reviewing phase. Many students find this phase difficult; they will often react against it initially and may not appreciate the benefits until much later in the course or after they have left. Experiential learning in general often has a time-lag. Because the experience can have a powerful emotional effect it tends to be remembered and can be revisited long after the event with understanding or illumination occurring then, in a way that is not characteristic of learning from a book or a lecture. When using student comments for evaluation purposes this long time-scale needs to be taken into account.

Debriefing of group activities is important and can help the students see the significance of their collective experiences. 'De-roling' as an essential part of debriefing role-play in particular is essential, yet is often neglected. However, it is helpful – as for all learning experiences – to allow 'loose ends' in group-work and not to try and draw out all the recognizable issues that the group seems unaware of. Tying loose ends can close down the learning: the overall effectiveness of the experience can be reduced in this way by an over-anxious tutor. There should be questions remaining, to serve as stimulants for students to work on in their thoughts and to motivate them to follow up later.

How should we assess?

One central issue is that higher education has traditionally assessed work individually. We are now in the process of changing the rules by also requiring students to be assessed on their ability to work cooperatively.

We should be clear about the extent to which we require this, or whether it is acceptable for students to produce alternative work individually.

Assessment of group-work is admittedly tricky. All too often, a great deal of effort is expended on the very small percentage contribution made to overall assessment by a particular group mark. This can become an unnecessary quest for unobtainable accuracy.

As for all assessment, it is important to set clear, published criteria at the beginning of an assignment. In the case of group-project work students should be made aware as to whether the criteria give precedence to the 'product' (for example a group report) or the learning and process management that go towards this. This is likely to affect the way the group works.

There can be real problems in assessing an individual's contribution to a group effort, in terms of the outcome, the content learned, the process skills of achieving the task and the interpersonal skills used within the group. Many innovative schemes are being devised to overcome this but there are still difficulties. Some we suspect are insurmountable. It is not simply a case of devising a better assessment form. There is a basic inconsistency which needs to be recognized, between requiring good teamwork and assessing individual performance. There may also be times when sublimation of individual aspirations is necessary for a good team performance, in which case individual assessment can seem unfair.

Peer assessment of group-work can give an important alternative view to tutor assessment of what actually went on in the group. But with the social pressures, lack of experience of the students and subjectivity, this does not remove all the problems. There is a need to offer training for students in self- and peer assessment, and to use a progression of exercises so that confidence can be gained in the processes involved. Peer assessment should not be seen as opting out by the tutor, who still has responsibility for the final mark, however it is derived.

The use of competences for individual work, with emphasis on behaviour, would seem to be a way forward for part of an individual's assessment. This encourages the individual to be a partner in the assessment process by identifying well-defined performance criteria and collecting evidence to establish that they have been achieved. This can be coupled with individual reflection on the task and on the process by which it was achieved, allowing a genuinely individual grading to be attempted.

It is important to distinguish between the use of summative and formative assessments. Formative assessment is generally more useful for actual learning purposes than is summative. As formative assessment gives feedback which does not contribute to the final marks used for a course, it is very often appropriate for group-work, allowing an improved learning situation to be created. It is also particularly relevant for assessing process skills and facilitating personal skills development. It may be possible to reduce drastically the quantity of summative assessment for a course so that only that which is essential for grading is carried out.

Students themselves can often become disillusioned by personal skills teaching which may offer far more than it can deliver. Students find that many of these skills take a long time to develop and are often highly contextual. In different circumstances the skill performance can change and sometimes virtually disappear. The extent and scope of transferability is rarely addressed in the literature produced by practitioners. Assessment of group and personal skills often involves assumptions about transferability which have yet to be substantiated. The need for context and variety of performance of skills must be acknowledged. Without proper care this situation could lead to a devaluing of the assessment process in these areas.

Assessment can easily work against learning by an over-emphasis on the 'right' answer or method or attitude. It is a common experience that we learn a great deal when things go wrong, yet in course assignments we often penalize 'mistakes'. This is particularly true in project and group-work which can be highly task-focused. If assessment rewards are always for a 'right first time' approach this will discourage the kind of risk taking and experimentation which are at the very heart of learning. It would be refreshing to see new assessment procedures developed which give more credit to risk, reflection and correction. Less assessment would then be based on final product quality, with its assumption that this correlates with quality of learning. More credit would be related to the learning that has taken place as a result of the task.

What about the students?

Students need to have positive group experiences before they can begin to use groups really effectively. Those that find group-work difficult need to be reassured and given sufficient variety in delivery to keep them motivated and able to learn. Some students can feel 'controlled' by group-work as with any other method; much depends on the attitude of the tutor.

The actual content of the group-work is particularly relevant: students need to see a group project as a real problem, worth solving and motivating in itself. They need to be able to relate the activity to reasons for studying at university and not as an irrelevance. The degree of perceived 'reality' can mean success or failure.

We must recognize that for some students group-work is very stressful. It can produce overwhelming anxiety which in turn demotivates and destroys the ability to learn in a given situation. Courses must be carefully planned to take account of the way group-work affects the student's programme and that the student is not involved in too many groups simultaneously. Switching from group to group, with the complexities of the social interaction involved, can be very demanding. So can the conflicting demands of group meetings interspersed with the more traditional course based on lectures and tutorials.

Written personal reflections, such as learning logs, are often used for assessment. In such cases we must address the ethical question of how much personal developmental work we should expect a student to make public or even to undertake. Demands in this area can easily impinge on personal freedom and the right to be an individual.

How much should we be involved in assessing personal attributes which go beyond those which are considered necessary for learning? Where is the line between helping students to obtain and reach their potential in employment and helping to create well-behaved clones for industry and commerce? Creativity does not always come from groups and can come from the non-conformist individual who needs the space to learn on his or her own. We must be careful we do not assent too readily to what industry thinks it needs and lose individuality in the worthy quest for good team-workers. We also need to encourage the kind of dissent and seeking after truth which can get squashed by the need of a group to complete the task. Individual enquiry and challenge of accepted concepts must remain an essential part of higher education.

What about the tutors?

Introducing group-work implies a significant change in the way the tutor operates. This change can make a considerable difference to the degree of satisfaction experienced by individual lecturers. The skill of performance, as for the lecture, is replaced by the skill of facilitation. The writing of course material assumes more importance. The necessary critical analysis of material is best achieved with teams of tutors working together in production and delivery. Learning objectives for group project-work have to be very carefully written and communicated to the students. Assessment methods and criteria must be rigorously examined and well understood by students and tutors. The course development phase becomes higher profile, since during the learning event itself there will usually be less obvious feedback/correction opportunities than in lecture/tutorial situations. Course evaluation using student feedback also becomes more important, with a need to listen carefully to what the students have actually experienced. This is often surprisingly different from the experience intended by the course team.

The acquisition of skills for managing groups needs to be an integral part of the training and development of lecturers. This means an understanding of the way groups work, the degree of structure necessary in given circumstances and the way to achieve positive learning outcomes through using group-work. There is a need for tutors to experience personally similar situations to those in which they will put students during the assignments they will run, and for tutors to begin to understand group processes and the strong feelings that can be engendered in groups.

The danger is that high contact hours and high stress levels will result in staff looking for techniques that will only solve their immediate problems, and that they themselves will settle for a solely surface approach to learning about groups. Time and space need to be made available if tutors are to adopt a deep approach to learning about groups as part of their own development.

While tutors need some understanding of the likely dynamics of groups before they use them in their teaching, most students are probably not helped by attempts at giving them information on this in the early stages. Students' own understanding of groups will be a part of their development, based on their personal experiences and experiences specifically designed into the course or courses. The exceptions to this are cases where group dynamics are part of the content of the course itself.

It is a weakness of some programmes to substitute group dynamics for structure. Students are not able to make use of understanding until they have had some practice. Group-work and open-ended problem solving require less tutor input but more course structure. It is a common experience that group-work demands a greater level of understanding of the learning process than more traditional learning methods. As so much else is open, less can be left to chance or free to interpretation.

Where are we going?

Group-work has reached an interesting point in higher education. The time is now past when it was innovative in its own right; we must now look for a sustained effort to improve the quality of group learning and assessment. For many courses there is opportunity to expand and convert group project-work into totally problem-based modules and programmes. We now need, however, to become more inquisitive about the student experience on the courses we offer, including the group-work element. The data obtained from evaluation and action research can be used positively to enhance the student learning experience in higher education.

Groups are unpredictable. This creates both the difficulties and the richness of experience for students and staff. We would regard as suspect any method of working with learning groups that gave prescriptive methods and guaranteed certain results. This book clearly demonstrates the variety of approaches which can be successful and that no one model approach would be adequate. As with most aspects of teaching, a great deal depends on the personality, skills and preferences of the tutor.

Tutors preparing for group-work need to come to terms with the complexities and uncertainties. Perhaps this is why it is not for everyone. We believe practitioners should be clear about their own learning philosophy and their values in group and personal interactions. Tutors need to address such issues as power, control, responsibility and their personal agenda as the building-blocks of their work. We believe that the concept of student-centredness in the work should be a core value.

The student-centred approach is based on a philosophy of teaching and learning that puts the learner centre-stage. The spotlight is on the needs, reactions and welfare of the learner, and away from the tutor. Student-centred learning seeks to improve the learning experience and its outcome by increasing motivation, through allowing and encouraging the learner to make more decisions about the learning process. It aims at improving quality by valuing and acting on the student's opinion of the learning process. It aims to produce 'life-long learners' by encouraging students to become independent, autonomous and to take responsibility for their own learning.

The outcomes expected from group-work should be realistic, recognizing that learning is an individualistic process, how little it can be controlled and that unanticipated outcomes may be just as valuable to the learner as those that the teacher sets up. If the values and the resources available are clear and helpful then we can relax about the outcomes. Intricate and challenging patterns of learning will take place. Tutors' inputs, environment, starting conditions and boundaries will affect the results. They will affect the areas of probability and possibility without defining definitive causal outcomes.

Each time we use group-based learning we undertake a new journey with exciting possibilities for all the learners involved, be they students or tutors.

References

Kolb, David A (1984) *Experiential Learning*, London: Prentice-Hall.

Further Reading

This is the editors' selection of some of the most useful books for practitioners of group-based learning in a higher education context.

Belbin, R M (1993) *Management Teams: Why they succeed or fail,* Oxford: Butterworth Heinemann.

Bion, W R (1961) *Experiences in Groups,* London: Routledge.

Boud, D (ed.) (1988) *Developing Student Autonomy in Learning,* London: Kogan Page.

Boud, D and Feletti, G (1991) *The Challenge of Problem Based Learning,* London: Kogan Page.

Boud, D *et al.* (eds.) (1985) *Reflection: Turning Experience into learning,* London: Kogan Page.

Bourner, T and Race, P (1990) *How to Win as a Part Time Student,* London: Kogan Page.

Brown, R (1988) *Group Processes – Dynamics within and between groups,* Oxford: Basil Blackwell.

Burnard, P (1989) *Teaching Interpersonal Skills – A handbook of experiential learning for health professionals,* London: Chapman and Hall.

Douglas, T (1991) *A Handbook of Common Groupwork Problems,* London: Tavistock/Routledge.

Gibbs, G and Habeshaw, T (1989) *Preparing to Teach,* Bristol: Technical and Educational Services Ltd.

Guirdham, M (1990) *Interpersonal Skills at Work,* London: Prentice-Hall.

Heron, J (1989) *The Facilitators' Handbook,* London: Kogan Page.

Jaques, D (1991) *Learning in Groups,* London: Kogan Page.

Johnson, D W and Johnson, F P (4th edn) *Joining Together – group theory and group skills,* New Jersey: Prentice-Hall.

Knapper, C and Cropley, A J (1985) *Lifelong Learning and Higher Education,* London: Kogan Page.

Larson, C E and LaFasto, F M J (1984) *Teamwork – What must go right, what can go wrong?,* London: Sage.

Lindsay Jnr., C W (1988) *Teaching Students to Teach Themselves,* London: Nicholas/Kogan Page.

Long, D G (1990) *Learner Managed Learning,* London: Kogan Page/St Martin's Press.

Miles, M B (1959/81) *Learning to Work in Groups,* Teachers College, Columbia University, USA.

Oxford Centre For Staff Development (1989) *Certificate in Teaching in Higher Education by Open Learning,* London: TES/Harper and Row.

Pfeiffer, J W (ed.) (1991) *Theories and Models in Applied Behavioural Science Vol. 2 – Groups,* Didcot, Oxon: Pfeiffer and Co.

Raaheim, K, Wankowski, J and Radford, J (1991) *Helping Students to Learn,* Guildford: Society for Research into Higher Education.

Ramsden, P (1992) *Learning to Teach in Higher Education,* London: Routledge.

Rogers, C (1983) *Freedom to Learn for the '80s,* New York: Merrill/Macmillan.

Slavin, R et al.(eds) (1985) *Learning to Co-operate, Co-operating to Learn,* New York: Plenum.

Storey, R (1989) *Team Building: A manual for leaders and trainers,* London: BACIE.

Taylor, B (no date) *Experiential Learning – A framework for group skills,* Leeds: Oasis Communications.

Topping, K (1988) *The Peer Tutoring Handbook – Promoting co-operative learning,* Beckenham: Croom Helm.

Weil, S W and McGill, I (eds) (1989) *Making Sense of Experiential Learning: Diversity in theory and practice,* Guildford: Society for Research into Higher Education.

Williams, T (1991) *Effective Debriefing: The Key to Learning,* London: BACIE.

Woodcock, M (1989) *50 Activities for Team Building,* Aldershot: Gower.

Zander, A (1982) *Making Groups Effective,* San Francisco, CA: Jossey-Bass.

Index